Children Talking
Politics

Children Talking Politics

Political Learning in Childhood

OLIVE STEVENS

Martin Robertson · Oxford

First published in 1982 by
Martin Robertson & Company Ltd.,
108 Cowley Road, Oxford 0X4 1JF

British Library Cataloguing in Publication Data

Stevens, Olive
    Children talking politics. — (Issues
    and ideas in education)
    1. Children and politics
    2. Political socialisation
    I. Title   II. Series
    306'.2 (expanded)   JA76
    ISBN 0-85520-489-3
    ISBN 0-85520-492-3 Pbk

Typeset in 10 on 12 point AM Photosetter Times by
Photosetting & Secretarial Services Limited, Yeovil
Printed and bound in Great Britain by Billings, Worcester

To my Family

Contents

Preface

This book starts from a particular view of childhood, the factual view of children living in the real world of work, communication, mass-media, mobility, prices and politics – and taking a lively and positive interest in it. Which is to say they are neither prisoners of fairyland, nor of adult beliefs that 'pretend' games are necessarily more interesting to them than what you can get a computer to do, what the day's news is about, or what it is for someone to have a right to something.

We tend to ignore this aspect of children's thinking, for we are largely unaware of it. In this book I have been concerned with demonstrating its existence. Much of the book is readily accessible to the non-specialist, interested in the ways in which children approach and use social and political ideas, while students of politics, child development, or teachers in training will find links with established work in these fields.

Why write this particular book? I would answer by pointing to the lack of material in the field, indeed the absence of a 'field' as such, at present, and the consequent need for some pioneering contributions. By the same token, no early look at a particular landscape can take in all its detail, or offer the definitive map of it. So while I am raising some questions about children's political understanding, learning and education, I am not working in terms of definitions and solutions. Rather, the book presents an account and interpretation of a range of children's political ideas and language, and, hopefully, a reference-point for the reader's own observations.

O. M. Stevens
1982

Acknowledgements

I would like to thank the people who have helped and encouraged me in various ways, at the various stages of producing this book. First the children, who talked to me, answered questions, wrote down their thoughts and shared their ideas. All this was made possible by the courtesy and co-operation of the Headteachers and staff who allowed me to go into their schools to carry out the project. My husband performed the tedious chore of typing the first draft, as well as giving me a constructive appraisal of it. I am also indebted to Robin Barrow for his practical advice and interest, and finally, towards the end of its journey, Kim Pickin's editorial assistance has smoothed some awkward corners in the manuscript, to its benefit.

1

Introduction

The idea of political education has gained some ground as an educational issue in recent years. There has been a growth of interest in exploring possibilities for curriculum development in schools and colleges, in approaches to the subject matter and in teaching methods. The reasons for this growth of interest are complex. They seem to connect with our increasing awareness that to describe an action as 'political' is not simply to label it, but to bring a particular range of insights and ideas to understanding what it means.

Study of the ways in which children gain these insights and ideas can serve several purposes. It can provide information of general interest, usable by parents and teachers; it can enable comparisons to be made between what happens here and in other countries such as the United States, where most of the existing research has been carried out. For purposes of teaching, generally, it may add some potentially useful information to the debate on the need for political education, in terms of what is possible for children at particular stages in education.

This book is about the ways in which children, between the ages of seven and eleven, are able to think about politics. As a result of engaging over 800 children in a variety of responses, it presents the view that during these years not only do children gain political concepts, but that these concepts develop through identifiable stages. The model of cognitive growth used for reference is Piaget's, and the emphasis is on children's active construction of political ideas.

According to Piagetian theory, to have a concept is to have grasped a principle and to be able to apply it. Practical activity becomes, for children, 'internalised' to form new mental structures or to change and extend existing ideas, which then continue to develop as they interact with stimuli from the environment. The important point to be made here is the importance and significance of early experiences for the

1

concepts that develop later. From the earlier experiences are constructed not only ideas but mental categories, to which new ideas are added as children find them appropriate, and so the categories of understanding expand. The ability to classify will govern this process. So a child's ability to classify anything as 'political' will indicate that he already has some kind of mental category and basis for deciding what it is for something to be 'politics'.

Why start observing children at seven for political concepts? I do not wish to suggest that political concepts suddenly appear with the seventh birthday, overnight. Nonetheless we must surely accept that before that age few children are likely to have sufficient communication skills to indicate them. This limitation concerns not only literacy, but language and thinking. A child may not understand the use of words in a question, or what is expected as a response to it, and even children under seven who show verbal ability are unlikely to have sufficient length of concentration for any discussion to develop. The seven-year-old stage, then, is taken to represent a threshold – which is reflected in our educational system – of the earliest point at which it may be possible to study the dawning of abilities to understand and express political meanings. Starting from this seven-year-old stage, the seven to eleven age-range is wide enough to accommodate the notion of 'development' in political concepts, and Piaget's model gives terms of reference and structure for its study.

Accepting this view of learning leads to questions of the 'inputs' available to children from their surroundings. What are their existing ideas to interact with, in terms of politics? The wider, public environment provides, in day-by-day events, usable information and vicarious experiences, and presents a sphere of action for children to identify, identify with, and learn to make judgements about. Over a period of time, such judgements might be expected to change in important respects. The nature and directions of such change is a crucial area for study, for it is on this basis that the notion of development can be founded. Discussion of the kind of knowledge involved, and some account of what it is for a child to have a political concept, to use it, and to understand a political idea, seems necessary. These are the kinds of questions that are investigated here, largely through the examination of children's own words.

This is essentially a study of children in action cognitively, thinking and communicating. In order to explore these processes and relate them to politics, I have made use of some relevant modern contributions to theory in these areas, which has given me a referential base, and helped to bring out the full significance of what the children had to say. The referential base is presented in chapter two.

Chapter three begins my presentation of the empirical work, looking first at children talking about politics. Their verbal responses to questions and the conversations that arise from these are re-created. The invitation is to listen, as children talk, argue, and work out ideas in small groups, at all ages between seven and eleven.

In chapter four the focus of interest changes to the written responses given by the children to questions which require short and specific answers, and comparisons are shown between the ways in which children at seven, nine and eleven deal with the same questions. Working in this way, it is possible to involve large numbers of children. So this section provides the 'spread' of information that enables me to trace the ways in which different age-groups understand certain ideas, and to suggest that some measure of generalisation is possible.

Chapter five discusses the nature of the children's understanding of politics on the evidence of all the information presented, and relates this to the initial body of theory. At this stage it is possible to identify some of the factors that seem to influence children's developing political concepts, and some of these, I shall argue, merit our continuing interest for the broad implications they have for children's learning. Their competence in verbal skills is one such issue, and another is the nature and effects of the informal learning available in our society via the media, particularly television. This medium which, in entertaining or informing children, presents them with social and moral inferences and pre-suppositions as settings for action, is difficult to evaluate in terms of the influence it has on a variety of attitudes and values. It may, however, be rather more easily considered for its influence on the processes of acquiring ideas and forming concepts, particularly in the political and social spheres. Perhaps it is appropriate to question whether television has an enabling function for the development of some kinds of concepts; if so, can we recognise it?

Chapter six, after presenting my conclusions in these areas, goes on to look at some of the implications that arise, out of the data collected for this work, for education at the Primary stage. The educational implications are an aspect that increased in importance, for me, as the research progressed. I have become aware, not only of some things that children are interested in and able to do, but of dimensions in their thinking that education, as we conceive of it and provide it, seems not to connect with.

I have learned whatever has become apparent to me through the unfailing courtesy of a great many children, who have been good enough to explain their ideas and share their thoughts with me. Children take easily to talking about politics. So easily, that the question of how they have become able to work with some of its basic ideas, in so short a time, must constantly occur to the observer. It is a fundamental question, and can only adequately be approached through understanding of the children's achievements at different ages. My first concern, then, must be to present the evidence for this, in some detail, before turning to discuss the capacity for political understanding. I am suggesting that this exists, as a distinct human attribute, not created by external circumstances, but responding to them; which is to imply some kind of genetic 'pre-programming' for constructing and using political concepts.

If we agree with Aristotle that we are 'political animals', it will be no more than we would expect for our children to have a 'ducks-and-water' relationship with political ideas, or for us to accept that active political learning takes place from an early age. This presents children in a very different role from that of mere passive recipients of political socialisation.

2

Raising the questions

The claim that even quite young children develop political concepts, and are capable of thinking about politics, involves me initially in giving a brief account of what I take that thinking to be. 'Thinking about' something is a continuing process. It involves not only having information and ideas, but using these to reach intermediate conclusions whose function, when reached, is to become obsolete, turning into points of departure for fresh insights. It is crucial, for any discussion of political learning or political education, to make a distinction between this kind of mental activity and the growth of uncritical attachment to factions or leaders, or country. I am not intent on presenting the view that every small boy and girl is, as W. S. Gilbert put it:

> '... either a little Liberal,
> Or else a little Conservative....'

Nor do I wish to trace what it is that makes people come to have patriotic feelings, or become politically socialised into supportive attitudes towards systems of government. These are important areas, of considerable interest, but they do not give us an exhaustive account of what politics is. For such an account, and to find out why the important areas mentioned are only partial accounts of politics as a sphere of human activity, we need to consider its widest connotation. Aristotle thought that political philosophy should concern itself with the whole of human behaviour, as well as the individual's relationship to the state. Accepting this as a principle, and getting from it a working basis for discussions with children, is to use those aspects of human behaviour that children can recognise as having something to do with the relationship of the individual to the state. It is also to involve children in deciding what shall be included in discussion, and to accept

5

that different age-groups may well use different connotations of what 'politics' is concerned with, in its essentials.

Examining children's thinking about politics, then, will mean looking at the ways in which they arrive at conclusions on such matters as the functions of government, their expectations of government, their perception of social principles, and the ways these are expressed in different parties' policies. In other words, we are dealing with the kinds of ideas children are capable of having at different ages, and their abilities to organise them logically.

Given that the broad aspects of politics listed above can be understood in greater or lesser degrees of complexity, it becomes clear that politics, as a way of understanding the world, allows for the notion of conceptual development. And also that comparisons can be made between the ways in which children develop political concepts, and other kinds of thinking. Relating political learning with a theory of cognitive development raises issues that need to be expressed in terms of the theory. Using Piaget's model and relating it to children's political thinking gives me scope to formulate a set of questions and through them to start exploring some of the issues, and raise any further questions.

First, does the pattern of children's development in political thinking follow that of their development of logical thought, as Piaget describes this? If the general patterns are found to be similar, a further question arises: are the stages in the development of political concepts reached at the same approximate ages as those Piaget identified as 'stages' in the development of logical and mathematical thinking? From questions of what happens, and when, we move on to consider how concepts come to be built, and it is here that Piaget stresses the vital importance of practical activity. Do political concepts arise from practical experience, as in early mathematical learning, or do language and verbal communication play a substantial, possibly stronger, role? The nature of political learning may permit of a number of contributary agencies and events, and it is possible that some of these have yet to be identified.

Considering the learners themselves is of primary importance in any learning situation, and individual differences are bound to be significant; but we do not yet know what kind of significance personal characteristics will have. We might want to ask whether there is such a thing as aptitude, or talent, for political learning, or whether different abilities in other areas influence what a child is able to do in politics.

Some of the accepted factors that influence other kinds of learning, such as sex, social grouping, self-concept and previous learning are obvious candidates for scrutiny in terms of their possible effect on political learning, but others may need to be investigated, or better understood. If we are to extend the list, how significant are factors in a child's experience such as formal relationships, social relationships, personality-type and habitual ways of relating with authority?

The concern to elucidate, and possibly further complicate, aspects of these questions provides my continuing rationale. The first stage will be to justify the link with Piaget's work, and clarify what is meant by the notion of developing political concepts. So it is both useful and relevant at this point to review in summary Piaget's ideas, which I shall be accepting as a general frame of reference.

PIAGET'S THEORY OF COGNITIVE DEVELOPMENT AND ITS RELEVANCE FOR POLITICAL LEARNING

Progressive adaptation is, for Piaget, the essence of intelligent behaviour. Its functions consist of understanding and inventing, in response to the nature of the environment. Development, in these terms, progresses through four main stages. In each stage a child's thinking is different in quality, not only from adult thinking, but from the kind of thought characteristic of the other stages in development.

The first stage of development Piaget calls the stage of 'sensori-motor' intelligence, which lasts from birth until 18 months or two years. This is followed by the 'pre-operational' stage, which lasts until a child is six or seven. There are two sub-stages in this period, the 'pre-conceptual' and the 'intuitive' stages of thought. The latter I have taken as the starting-point for the purposes of this study. (And I am, of course, using a skeletal outline of Piaget's work, of which further reading is essential for the student.)

During the period of sensori-motor intelligence a child's achievements concern his abilities to manipulate objects in space and time, and to see simple causal connections between them. From the age of about two to seven these abilities are transferred to the symbolic and verbal planes. Symbolic thinking, or the ability to represent one thing by another, enables a child to use language, to interpret and draw pictures, to extend his abilities in play in symbolic or constructional games, and later to read and write. Thus his range and speed in thinking increases, especially as language develops.

In response to stimuli received, the processes Piaget terms 'assim-ilation' and 'accommodation' interact and enable a child to extend his thinking and produce intelligent behaviour adapted to his environ-ment. Change in environment, or increased perception of it, will result in progressive adaptation. At seven, logical reasoning is not usually possible, for a child is not yet able to regard experiences from any point of view except his own, and this egocentrism is a stumbling-block to the reversability of reasoning that logic requires.

During the third stage, of 'concrete operations', a child becomes, by the age of eleven or twelve, capable of reversing an operation mentally but only as an extension of his 'concrete' experiences. As his perceptions become 'de-centred' instead of egocentric, he becomes able to link ideas and relate them to each other. Understanding of relationships, such as principles and examples of them, also develops. The physical facts in any situation are still the basis of his thinking, and will be until the stage of 'formal operations' is reached in adolescence, when objective and abstract reasoning is achieved, as the fourth and final stage in development.

Possessing concepts enables a child to bring order out of his experience by understanding similarities between events and objects which appear on the surface to be different. For example, once he has the concept 'dog' he can classify a variety of creatures of differing size, shape, colour and temperament as dogs, and he will react to them in a similar way. The aspects of a concept that change with cognitive development include:

(a) its validity, by which is meant the degree to which a child's understanding of the concept matches that of the larger social community. As children develop, the meanings of concepts gain in similarity for all children, and so become more valid in the sense of being more general and usable;

(b) its status, or the extent to which it can be articulated and the child can use it in his thinking;

(c) its accessibility, that is to say, the ease with which a child can talk about his ideas and produce them in reasoning.

Existing concepts provide a framework into which new information can be absorbed, provided it can be understood by a child. Thus it either matches, or is only a little in advance of, his existing ideas. This kind of connecting, of the known to the new, makes assimilation, understanding, and therefore learning, possible. As a process, it can take place either through play, or through other undirected activities and associations, or through the directed thinking that occurs when a child tries to solve a given problem.

In spite of the fact that so much in politics is problematic in the sense of being permanently contestable, the basic principles for solving problems or clarifying issues apply at least as much to politics as any other area of discourse. Comprehension of events is involved, as is the ability to come to logical conclusions and understand the reasons for the steps taken in reaching them. These are basic requirements for logical political thought which distinguish it from merely reacting or holding unexamined beliefs and opinions.

However, a child, if he is to think flexibly and be able to re-arrange his ideas in response to circumstances, needs more than habits of thought. He needs to have insights, which I distinguish from mere beliefs or opinions by virtue of two conditions. The first is that an insight has relevance and direction: it is a move towards a hypothesis. The second condition is that an insight is scrutinised. To use his insights, an individual needs an internal critical faculty, enabling him to evaluate his own thinking and, when necessary, discard an idea. The capacity to so examine one's own thinking will come, according to a Piagetian account, when the individual becomes able to 'de-centre' his thinking from his own viewpoint and construct other points of view.

WHAT IS INVOLVED IN EARLY POLITICAL LEARNING?

In terms of developmental psychology, the mental processes under consideration as relevant to political learning are: firstly, encoding, or giving selective attention to one event or aspect of a situation rather than another, and interpreting the relevant information. The encoding process is directly related to age, and to individual selectivity of attention. By the age of eight, the dramatic increase in a child's capacity for sustained attention which occurs between five and seven years of age will have been completed, enabling his performance on lengthy tasks to improve in quality (see Mussen, Conger and Kagan 1969).

The second process involves memory functions, which can be expected to improve during middle childhood. Differences in memory between children of the same age appear to be related to the ability to sustain attention, the availability of language, concepts and images associated with events that help to 'fix' them in memory, and to variations in motivation. Retrieval of information from memory demands some effort, and a factor here will be whether the child is motivated to go on searching for further information in his memory store, after the first, easily accessible layer is obtained. Variables here are demonstrated during some of the discussions with children, and it could be considered that a first political discussion provides a unique opportunity to observe the motivational level of children in this area. For in responding to a new set of stimuli, a child decides for himself how far he is willing to engage his skills and memory.

Thirdly, evaluative abilities can also be expected to develop with other intellectual skills. Some children display an impulsive style of hypothesising, accepting their own first ideas as a basis for action. Others may take considerably longer, and reject several ideas before producing a final satisfactory version. These different attributes may also help to determine how easily a child will be able to accept, or reserve judgement on, the ideas of others, and in this sense will be significant for the development of his political thinking.

The notion of a child constructing his or her world is basic to Piaget's account of mental development. Children build not so much a 'world-view' as areas of reference for themselves: so mathematics, space, time and so on come into existence for them as they acquire concepts through experiences of these areas. Once achieved, the concepts are put to work, classifying and organising further experience. As a result, concepts expand, refine, become more specialised or more diverse, and networks of concepts are built up. In other words, children, through the experiences available to them, construct particular kinds of intelligence and states of consciousness.

The question that parents, teachers or any interested adults might want to ask is whether all this is bound to remain invisible and inaccessible to an observer. Or are there ways of understanding *what* is happening *while* it is happening?

To some extent, children's states of consciousness do become accessible to observation, largely through their own accounts of what is significant for them. In some areas of learning children provide active accounts of the significant; they do things, repeat them, do something differently, try again, involve somebody else, often at an early age when play is alongside others rather than with them, without a word being spoken. Physical exploration, building with blocks, making mud pies, water-play, all provide active accounts of stages in understanding. The next stage will be for a child to be able to give a verbal account of his activities, and adult interest can become a catalyst, helping his thinking by asking the questions that bring his experiences together, into the realisation – when he is ready for it – of principles. To ask 'How was it done? How did you think of that? Is there a different way? What will you do with it next?' is to enter into a child's ways of experiencing, in a manner that observation without the discussion of what has been done, doesn't provide.

Does this apply to political learning? Verbal interactions have a function here, in bringing together different kinds of experiences: the 'in-school' direct experiences of structures, group involvement, rules and authority; notions of fairness, democratic procedures and so on with the second-hand, reported experience about the outside world of politics and events. For political learning a child's verbal account of what is significant or interesting for him will reveal the closest points of contact between his own experience and the wider realities. Usefully, it will also provide the generative ideas and words from which further gains might be expected to develop and which can point the way towards effective teaching and learning. Thus a child's perception of relationships between political roles leads him to the awareness of political structures and some appreciation of purposes and ends. As this is achieved, there will also be the conceptual basis for further political understanding.

The broad context for new perceptions is the general awareness of the political world, existing at some distance but occasionally brought much closer, as at times of heightened political activity. It is thus recognised, conceptualised, and political content classified as a category of information and reference. This is not to suggest, returning to the seven-year-olds, that small children, to have concepts of politics must be capable of sophisticated classification or abstract thought, but rather that it is not necessary that they should be. What is at stake is the nature of a 'political' concept.

Politics is not an abstract concept, but a class of activities that can be grasped in terms of its intermediate ends, rather than in theoretical terms. A significant point in the discussion of concept formation is that political concepts have a particular construction. An activity becomes a political activity by virtue of the ends to which it is directed: it has a strongly intentional dimension. In these terms, many kinds of concepts are potentially political concepts. To recognise them it is necessary to understand what something means in a political context: in other words, how it can be used for achieving certain kinds of purposes.

When that class of purposes can be recognised, the idea of something not directly involved in processes, but having political connotations, can be understood.

Prior to the understanding of this kind of potentially political concept is an understanding of the directly political kind. These concepts refer to the institutions and processes of government, and to organising principles. Understanding of the content of the principles may well be present, for a child, when the ability to give definitions causes difficulty, and this can lead to some misunderstanding. For if we were to insist on a child being able to answer exhaustively the question, 'What is politics?', as the necessary condition for accepting that he has a concept of politics, there would be a danger of avoiding the real issue, of ignoring any ability or interest he may have in discussing the activities and issues which constitute politics.

If a child has such abilities and interests then he possesses political concepts and also the concept of politics as an area of human behaviour, though his capacity to define or analyse the word remains incomplete. And, as with politics, so with other concepts such as freedom, democracy, having rights, governing, having political parties and competing policies, treating people equally – the list is not exhaustive. If children are able to enter into discussion of these ideas, putting points of view and using examples to explain their meanings, some concepts are clearly present, albeit in an early stage of development, and based on simple personal experience.

Piaget's system deals consistently with the practical and enactive side of cognitive growth and his account of concept formation is the most comprehensive that we have, as yet. In common with Bruner (1973), Piaget emphasises 'knowing' as construction, and stresses the essentially active role of the learner. This is in contrast to stimulus-response theories of learning which, in the restricted view they present of the learner and the learning process, do not describe satisfactorily the explorative nature of concept-building in politics.

THE CENTRAL ROLE OF LANGUAGE IN THE DEVELOPMENT OF POLITICAL CONCEPTS

Observation of children's play and free interactions can provide almost endless clues to the ways they think about matters that we connect with basic issues of social and political philosophy. The clues present us with questions to consider, and this can be instanced by watching children at play. What is involved, for them, in accepting the rules of a game? Are these understood as 'given', i.e. as pre-existing and inflexible, as the ancients thought of natural law? If so, who discovers them and who knows them? The leaders of the group? The owner of the ball or bat or whatever? Or everybody? Or are the rules decided upon by the group, and if so, how? Who decides how? What is involved in some children gaining prestige and emerging as leaders over a period of time and in other children not only consenting but contributing to this process?

Taking another aspect, what rights do children claim, in relation to each other and to adults? What sense do they make of the notion of obligation? How is it possible for an observer to begin to look for enlightenment on these kinds of questions?

Two possibilities come to mind. An observer might be able to remain in contact with a group on a long-term basis, ready to monitor or record any spontaneous behaviour that he found interesting. But in this case his presence would serve to modify that behaviour and, unless the groups were very small, few interactive situations could be fully appreciated or understood. Furthermore, this type of observation might in practice only be possible for the person teaching them, in contact with the same class of children for a school year.

Another possibility is to conduct a classroom debate or discussion with children. However, this approach tends to produce disappointing results in practice, often due to the relationship between quality of discussion and numbers of children. The more children present, the larger a non-participant 'audience' becomes, and the less willing anyone becomes to experiment with words or ideas or to risk real communication.

To achieve communication and the quality of discussion that works through children becoming interested and involved, a third method seems necessary; that of working with a small group of individuals, and talking with them. Thus the emphasis reverts back to using language, and to individual children, rather than observing group behaviour from a distance.

In this study the small-group discussion, as a style of communication, occupies a central position. It is important for two main functions: in providing the most direct way of examining children's thinking about politics – and asking them questions about what they say – and in creating a situation with its own dynamics. Once started, the demands of discussion and other children's contributions, serve to organise a child's political ideas and bring them into use. The ideas might be about concepts or be made possible through a child's having concepts, so what is being organised and presented in discussion might equally be described as a child's political consciousness.

THE LANGUAGE OF POLITICAL IDEAS

Politics differs, in terms of the demands it makes upon language, from those areas of the social sciences that seem to be characterised by innovatory use of language. The basic vocabulary of politics is embedded in ordinary usage and so it will follow that for children to develop political concepts ordinary language will suffice, initially, at least. It provides the words, gives them some context and reference, and makes possible some general accounts of politics in non-specialist ways. To illustrate: politicians, like everyone else, 'meet' 'talk' 'ask' 'tell' 'make up their minds' and 'look after' things. It is not until some elaboration is attempted that children need even the commonly used terms of politics. To achieve elaboration of basic ideas, a child's ability to become dissatisfied with the generality of his own language, and so attempt to re-organise it to accommodate new information and ideas would appear to be the most helpful attribute. In this way, the acquisition of more complex language, and more specific under-standing can be expected to reinforce each other.

The media's daily coverage of politics and current events provides a constant stimulus to this process. From this source, children may acquire not only information and images, but vocabulary organised into models of description, argument and discussion. Certainly for some children, these models seem to function as 'external amplifiers', in Bruner's sense, of their powers: they function as an 'external pull' which is as important to development as the corresponding 'internal push'.

For early political development, the notion of language-codes (Bernstein 1970, 1971) is a source of some pertinent and interesting questions. Accepting that a restricted language-environment may well act as a constraint on political concept-formation, the issue remains of exactly what it is that is being inhibited. Could any such process of constraint be analysed? If it does occur, might both political language and understanding of working-class children be different from that of middle-class children? This would not be merely a matter of holding different opinions and attitudes but would involve abilities to understand issues concerning relationships and abstractions. It can be further questioned whether some children might still be able, within a restricted language-code, to develop personal strategies for expressing ideas and developing them.

It would seem that, if Bernstein's conclusions regarding the effects for children of restricted access to language are carried to a logical conclusion, the process of concept-formation in politics may well be an area where some children are particularly vulnerable. For in the absence of 'concrete' activity in the 'concrete-operational' stage, language has a double task; that of formulating new concepts, and of rendering explicit any tacit political understanding a child may possess. If to refine a concept is for some tacit dimension of knowledge, in Polanyi's (1958, 1969) sense, to become explicit, the role of language can hardly be over-emphasised. These are some of the questions concerning language and politics that are considered in the following chapters and are related to children's own words.

PLAY: THE 'ENACTIVE' STAGE IN POLITICAL UNDERSTANDING

Through their play children construct an environment for themselves within the larger one of school. Here their ways of organising their chosen activities reflect some basic aspects of the political world. Groups are formed to pursue agreed objectives; alliances arise, often shifting dynamically towards minimal combinations – the 'best friend' syndrome, often more noticeable in girls' friendships than in boys' – and on this social basis certain principles are internalised. The principles concern choices. There is territory to be claimed and rights to it consolidated, new members to be admitted to the group, leadership roles to establish and relations with other groups, including the authorities, to formulate.

The problem for children's groups is basically how such decisions are to be reached. School training and innate needs for security work together to establish conformities that serve to reduce anxiety. But other factors act upon this balance. Awareness of personal identity brings a need for status and recognition within the group. Maintaining the group's stability, however, calls for a balancing of personal interests with co-operation: the willingness to accept a group definition of the general interest, so as to remain in a position to contribute to it. This tacit commitment is expressed in children's use of 'we', 'our' and 'us' when referring to the group, however small it may be. It seems to be a convention of childhood to reserve the use of names and individualised references for family, and to use generalised pronouns in reference to groups and group members. When this happens, the distinctions made concern not only individuals, but the awareness of different forms of life and of membership.

Children's needs for group membership concern their purposes for action, in that a group widens the sphere of possibilities for action. In play with others, a child is involved in ways of making choices and relationships, acceptance of a role and seeing the need for rules. Playing football is a case in point, requiring not only a ball and a number of players but some kind of organisation, however minimal. The alternative to accepting direction from outside is for the group to find its own working basis of co-operation. Finding this means that some of the basic procedures of democracy have to be invented, and this, in effect, is what happens. Principles of fairness are expressed in the ethic of not cheating, with its appropriate sanctions. This, with notions of equality and equal rights, requires implementation in all group activities. So children discover the ritual of voting, which supersedes earlier, cruder methods of choosing games or allocating roles.

Perhaps most important of all, the principle of having principles is discovered: that an ethical structure gives an ordered basis to activities, and consequent attachment to such a framework is developed. This can be seen in children's early intuitive attachment to rules, which is not abandoned at the concrete operational stage, but rationalised.

SEX DIFFERENCES IN PLAY

From observing their play activities, it is possible to conclude that girls develop less ability to perceive and make use of spatial relationships than boys. This affects the nature of their play: they are less attracted to exploring the possibilities of open spaces, preferring to consolidate small areas of 'personal space'. In this way their play and social interactions from an early age tend to take place on a smaller scale than those of boys; there is less emphasis on large-group activity, and consequently less need for finding ways of organising such activity and of keeping the members of the active group under normative control.

Groups of small boys come together most frequently for the purpose of making a football game, the scope and area of which is only limited by the size of the playground. This is a procedure independent of authority, needing only a ball as equipment, which is easily obtained. For girls, there is no comparable activity; a shared skipping rope, the hide-and-seek game, the individual hoops and balls do not provide a large-group situation, and rounders is not a general favourite. Netball, the established organised game for Junior school girls is a closely rule-governed activity that takes place within carefully defined spatial limits. The structures of the team games available for girls are so formalised that they are not easily transferable to the informal setting, of playtime in the playground. The question might well arise of why girls do not join the football or cricket groups, or play all-girls versions, if they need this kind of activity. The usual situation is that they do not in fact do so. While this may be in part due to the peer-group pattern of single-sex membership, which is rarely broken at the Primary stage, there is also the apparent factor of sex-linked preference for one type of play activity over another.

On the basis that different physical organisation of play takes place (Terman and Tyler 1954), it can be suggested:

(a)   that girls' social organisation results from this;

(b)   that such social organisation in turn leads to further differ-
      entiation in forms of play; for example, symbolic play might be
      expected to be more pleasurable to girls and therefore last
      longer as a developmental stage;

(c)   that an awareness of role rather than of structure is conse-
      quently likely to develop as a cognitive style, for girls, and that
      verbal abilities are likely to develop earlier for them than for
      boys.

Verbal interaction during play is a particularly valuable style of communication in that it is often unselfconsciously exploratory; however, during strenuous ball games it is likely to be brief and cliché-ridden, which indicates for many boys, a limiting of experience in this aspect of learning.

As a result of such differences in play and social organisation, and the language and interests that connect with them, the culture of the school resolves itself into the girls' culture and the boys' culture. At the deeper level two essentially separate environments exist, resulting ultimately in different ways of organising ideas and perceiving the world, which must have wide implications for political thinking.

EARLY SCHOOLING AS CONTEXT AND SOURCE OF
POLITICAL UNDERSTANDING

Children's understanding of freedom, authority and equality

The notion of freedom is a pervasive one in Primary education. There is
continuing debate concerning its nature, its intrinsic and extrinsic
value for education, its desirable extension and its applications. The
idea of freedom has close connections with what have come to be
regarded as morally right teaching methods. Values such as creativity,
critical thinking, that cultivation of the imagination which for a writer
such as Mary Warnock (1973) is the basis of quality in education, are all
considered by many teachers and theorists to be fostered by a
maximum of freedom in the classroom. Such freedom is actualised by
children 'learning by discovery', through organising their own projects
and being, to a large extent, free to choose their own tasks and methods
of pursuing them.

Interestingly little, if any, attention has been paid, educationally, to
the children's own attitudes to the concept of freedom as structured by
authority, or to their ideas about what constitutes a free situation, and
how much freedom is desirable, or indeed tolerable. The implicit
assumption of much 'progressive' theory in education is that freedom,
to a child, is an absolute; the basic problem being one of how to increase
it. This emphasis is to a large extent a reaction from nineteenth-century
modes of teaching children, when the emphasis in education lay on the
acquisition and storing of information, for which purpose memory
provided the basic intellectual tool, and harsh discipline the primary
motivation.

In moving away from this tradition, the present situation has
produced in our Primary schools, highly individual institutions. If the
'traditional-progressive' polarisation· is seen as a continuum, then
individual schools find their particular ethos somewhere between the
two extremes. Where exactly a school decides to 'settle', what
particular educational values it supports in terms of curriculum
content and teaching methods, are matters for each institution and
particularly for the Head Teacher to decide. The position of a Primary
Head Teacher is one of considerable power. He or she has no formal
obligation to involve staff or parents in decision-making in educational matters, or to run a school on democratic lines. In practice, a
high degree of co-operation and consultation exist in the majority of
schools: but they exist as the Head's policy.

The structure of power communicates itself to children at a very early age. Infants are quite aware that the Headmaster or Headmistress is the ultimate source of authority, and therefore that ultimate sources of authority exist. The internalisation of this concept is probably the most significant fact of early political socialisation, and it has taken place after a few weeks' attendance at the Infants school, that is, by the age of five. This is not to say that the Head will be feared or disliked; he or she may well be liked as a person. But children are aware that any interpersonal relationship is paralleled by their relationship with the role, and this is also true of their relationship with their class teacher. Concepts of authority structures are built most firmly by those teachers who use the 'Head-image' in support of their own authority, in other words, by the relatively insecure, and this fact also communicates itself to children.

The fact that some adults find the process of keeping children constructively occupied easier than others, means that class-control is a highly variable attribute between individual teachers. It is to a large extent a personality function. Accordingly, some teachers are able to exert a charismatic authority that needs to draw very little on the formal authority of the role. Others need to lean more heavily on this, and some find their actual authority in the classroom is less than that invested in their role: they find difficulty in actualising their formal authority.

Children have little difficulty in perceiving that the links in a chain of authority are not all of the same strength, and of using this fact in ways that seem appropriate and interesting to them. Testing or 'trying-out' of teachers' authority styles is part of any group's initial response to a new arrival, and such exploration of personality seems to be the social parallel to children's need to explore their environment physically. Conclusions are reached, experiences repeated, and concepts are formed concerning the nature, legitimacy, functions, flexibility and desirability of authority.

Closely linked with the notions of freedom and authority are the set of ideas that express themselves as expectations of the system: of justice and fairness, of equality of treatment, built on the necessary assumption of purposes that promote the general good. Children's concepts of fairness and equality, although manifestly linked to the idea of distribution of almost any commodity, that is, of equal shares, find difficulty in the idea of distributive justice applied on the basis of needs. That particular understanding of equality can be compared with perception of the Piagetian idea of 'conservation'. To apply it, capacities that enable children to free themselves from the 'here and now', and to realise that appearances can be deceptive, are necessary. What needs to be conserved is initial information; a child will need to be able to return to the beginning of his chain of thought and be able to assess what reasons are relevant when drawing conclusions. Efficiency here is not usually achieved until the age of eight or nine, and refers to concrete phenomena. The understanding of an abstract 'equality' which can perceive the variables in a situation, cannot be expected to develop until adolescence. So for this study, children's ability to use the ideas of equality is assumed to have practical limitations.

However, the idea of fairness, of having voices in discussion or equal rights, for example, to choose a game or activity, can be accommodated. This equality may be expressed democratically. Children choosing games in turn, or according to majority preference, reflect normal behaviour. It might be asked whether this is based on principles of equal sharing, leading to the intuitive democracy of 'one individual, one vote'. In practice, this seems to be what happens; the idea of sharing equally becomes the procedural principle, ritualised as part of the game.

Whether children develop any concept of a 'public good' is another question of interest. The possibility is necessarily circumscribed, for what aspects of a 'public good' would children identify in school, or isolate as instances? If they themselves, as a group, are to be the 'public' concerned, the questions become easier because they are linked to the satisfaction of needs. One of childhood's basic emotional needs is for the security of being able to regard authority as benevolent (Hess and Torney 1967). Experience of the 'helping' function of familiar authority, is transferred to public figures; the early expectations of 'helping us' become elaborated into the idea of legitimate obligations.

'Us' can mean either the small circle, or it can mean a child's identification with the larger community 'out there'. With this acceptance of overlapping worlds, comes the realization that certain people work in certain ways to 'help us': structures exist in order to serve the public good. On this basis it can be understood that ideas, goodwill, intentions and specific tasks, operate through institutions and networks. In a political sense, the concept of helping can be used in various contexts and situations, and it is one which children have no difficulty in transferring and approving. If politics and political figures 'help us', then they are in the 'our' interest; logically, there must exist a common interest to be served.

Children's understanding of rules and government

Children's concepts of the nature, purposes and justification of government are gained initially from the rule-governed situation in which they live, that is, the home and the school. The earliest socialisation by the parents is designed to produce socially acceptable behaviour in their children, and most children, by the age of school entry, have internalised the familial norms securely enough for the school to build on them. The school sets out to achieve institutionally acceptable behaviour by inculcating support for its own norms, for the processes of education need an ordered and disciplined environment, if they are to continue. The notion of what constitutes order and discipline is not at issue, for these are variables in Primary Schools. The area for consideration is children's ideas about rules and government.

These ideas about rules and government in the school are linked with children's ideas about justice and fairness, with their attitudes to authority and the acceptance of influence. They are linked also with children's ideas about freedom, its safe limits and its uses. A child's view of rule-keeping and its associated concepts is likely to influence his attitudes towards government in the political sense, as he develops towards cognitive maturity. His expectations of, and confidence in, the society in which he lives, in terms of its stability, principles and procedures will depend on the ways he relates to government. His view of these attributes will determine to a great extent the quality of his participation in them.

Do children rationalise and consciously support rule-keeping? Does the rationalisation, if it takes place, have any transfer to the idea of government on the national scale? It has been suggested by Piaget, that children's ideas on rule-keeping are linked with their developing capacity for making moral judgements and pass through cognitive developmental stages. Do their concepts of government develop significantly in this way between the ages of seven and eleven?

Kohlberg's (1971) suggestion that although the cultural content of moral beliefs differs, the development of their form is a cultural invariant, stresses uniformities in the ways in which children conceive of rules and internalise social principles. Initially, he claims, they see rules as functioning by power and compulsion. Later, rules are seen as a function of security: they become instrumental to the satisfaction of needs and can be used for gaining rewards. Progress thereafter is towards conceiving of rules as supporting some desirable end, and ultimately as principles connected with justice, supporting the accepted social order. Kohlberg's main point is that the sequence of levels of the understanding of rules is the basis of moral development, and that this development could not take place in any other sequential way because of the relationships of the concepts involved.

This is an interactionist position; maturation theories in moral matters are rejected, as is also the Kantian view that ways of understanding rules are 'moulds' into which experiences are fitted. Like Piaget and Bruner, Kohlberg insists that development occurs through the individual restructuring the ways in which he understands his environment. The question that remains is one of commitment; of how children become emotionally attached to principles, of the way in which the desire for justice, or the capacity for moral indignation, is awakened. Commitment might logically appear to be connected with the stage of being able to visualise some 'ideal' situation (for example, in which everyone was treated fairly) and will also become apparent in children's use of moral imperatives.

CHILDREN AND IDEOLOGICAL THINKING: THE PERCEPTION OF ALTERNATIVES IN POLITICS

The concept of ideology is an abstraction. Its comprehension involves the ability to grasp and to contrast alternative political and social arrangements, and to bring to this task some understanding of relevant criteria for judging systems of social priorities. Children's abilities to consider the world as it is and formulate alternatives of how it might be, belong in cognitive theory generally, to adolescence, as does the commitment to such choices.

What can be expected of the seven- to eleven-year-olds here? How do children come to perceive the possibility of alternatives in political affairs? In the period of concrete operations (the primary school age-range), children's ability to understand alternatives in Piagetian terms is assessed largely in terms of their ability to handle mathematical or spatial concepts. The understanding, for example, that a certain distance can be measured in any direction from a given point is one early achievement. At a later stage, children will discover, for example, that the view of a three-dimensional model of a mountain top will vary according to the position from which an observer looks at it.

The child's understanding of practical alternatives arises from his earliest opportunities to make choices. When he can handle the concept of choice, a child is ready to have his range of possible alternatives expanded. It can be argued that his needs then are not so much for 'freedom' to make his choices, as for appropriate information that will help him to make the judgements on which to base them.

To ask how a child is to acquire such information in order to make political judgements is to ignore the facts that children do acquire political information and do make judgements here. The quality of judgements, in terms of rationality and objectivity, will be a function of the development of a child's concepts of politics. The ability to be other than subjectively oriented, to be able, not only to arrange social and political priorities in time and space, but to visualise oneself as occupying two positions simultaneously, for example as a member of a small interest group and as a member of the larger community, is the political interpretation of the spatial model. Its end stage is an essential freedom of thinking from the 'here and now' socially, the transcending of the narrowly self-interested point of view.

Appropriate information for making judgements might be regarded as those experiences which help children to construct their political world on as broad a foundation as possible. The information itself flows from the environment, to be processed and categorised by children as it is received. The categorising process is likely to be limited to a narrow, or even single basis for judgements (for example, the conviction that politics is exclusively about prices), which will only be extended when children are able to structure relations between relations, or to make use of proportionality.

It has been suggested (Mealings 1963) that a mental age of at least thirteen is required before these mental processes are developed, and that more usually a mental age of fifteen or sixteen is necessary before the establishment of formal operational thinking. Ruth Beard (1969) points out that the differences in thinking are largely socially and educationally determined. It might usefully be added that the realm of discourse in which the thinking takes place is also of considerable relevance.

The comparison between the conceptual development which takes place in science and mathematics, and that which takes place in political thinking, has to take into account the particular attributes of political concept-formation. Not only has motivation a direct and personal bearing, but the mechanism of political processes ensures that from time to time the social life of the country is pervaded by intensified political campaigning. This occurs not only during a general election but at times of strikes, shortages or greater or lesser crisis. A general election is, of course, the strongest of these influences. Its presentation of alternative personalities, structures, priorities and criteria for the common good, presents conceptual models to which children are exposed, usually via the media, and which some of them find to be of interest.

It would be difficult to justify the disregarding of this exposure for cognitive development in politics. If there were to be, occasionally, a few weeks of highly intensified mathematical activity on the same scale, it could be expected to effect considerable differences in the general level of understanding and interest, even for those who had little or no previous experience of the subject. Add to this the immediacy of television news coverage and it is likely that some telescoping of certain aspects of Piaget's stages of cognitive development may occur. It is suggested that this telescoping does take place, particularly in intermittent periods of strong political activity, but that it also continues for those children who spend significant amounts of their leisure time watching television current affairs programmes or news.

It is not suggested that whatever is gained in this way is, in cognitive terms, operational. Children are not acquiring skills or knowledge. But they may well acquire the vocabulary and information useful to aid transfer and extension of limited social concepts to ideas that relate to the larger world and extend their perceptions of alternative social arrangements.

How interested are children in politics? Individual motivation and levels of interest are of obvious importance for any account of learning. However, political learning is outside the sphere of institutionalised motivation. So it might be considered that, given any political learning at all to have taken place for a child, he must have been interested in politics to that extent.

The affective, emotional dimension of understanding is neglected by Piaget, nor does he attach any vital importance to the ways in which a child's social environment affects learning. It is impossible to ignore these factors when considering early political learning. It would seem hardly possible for political concepts to develop or exist without reference to social and emotional, as well as cognitive, development. Unless, that is, the term 'political' were to be given a simple denotive, or 'naming' character. Its function, in that case, would be to enable children to put a mental label reading 'political' on institutions and procedures, with no comprehension of their purposes, moral structures or dynamics. This is not the sense in which I want to examine children's thinking about politics; rather, I hope to present their developing awareness of an important area of human purposes and commitments.

3

Talking about politics

We come to the point where the characters enter, and the preceding chapter falls into place as a background for children in action. To preserve anonymity I have given them fictitious names, indicated their localities only broadly and their schools not at all. None of this manages to blur the impact of their personalities or their styles of answering questions, or thinking aloud or arguing with each other, for these are conveyed by their personal language and turns of phrase, which are reported verbatim. Editing has taken the form of selecting from a plentiful harvest of material, and 'tidying-up' has been minimal, used either to free a child's contribution from too many 'Ummms...' or 'Wells...', or to break up the occasional five minute sentence, for ease of reading.

The discussion groups were set up during the school day, and children released from their normal class activities for the half-hour or so that it took to record the conversation. Having their discussions recorded, even in some cases video-recorded was, surprisingly, no distraction. Concentration was on the matter in hand. Numbers were flexible, so that there could be comparisons of what happened when as few as two, or as many as five children worked together, and the composition of groups was fairly haphazard. Children were told what I wanted to do, which was to hear about what they knew of politics, and they were invited to come and talk, in an empty classroom, or the school library or whatever space happened to be available in the school that day. Some came with their best friends, others because they had finished their maths, some because they didn't want to finish their maths just at the moment, and to most it probably seemed a reasonably interesting idea and a change from routine. There was no question of ability grouping or of selecting any particular type of personality. In this respect it seemed the mix was so varied that the children in any age-

26

group might have little in common apart from that. What they did prove to have in common, with very few exceptions, was what might be described as a practical interest in day-to-day events and politics: that is to say they knew what was going on in the world and had formed some opinions about events and personalities. They were ready to share and explain their opinions and defend them in argument.

My first concern was with finding out how much the children knew about politics, irrespective of how they had learned it. That came later. So the start was with facts; who the Prime Minister was, what happens in Parliament, how a person becomes an MP, and so on. But facts, to make sense, need to be used and connected, so the next stage was to see how far the children were able to do this. Encouraging them made for the kind of 'open-ended' discussion that isn't about finding answers to specific questions, but about exchanging ideas, putting forward points of view – and listening to what other people want to say.

We went into questions of what 'governing the country' is all about, what makes a 'good Prime Minister' – and what a bad one would be like – and what a political party is for. We compared the Queen's job with that of the Prime Minister and started to work with ideas of accountability, freedom and the rule of law. The unknown factor at this stage was whether the children would be able to cope at all with even the simplest questions about politics. Even adolescents have been presented, from time to time in the occasional media 'report' or small-scale 'survey', as almost totally uninterested and uninformed. And while this remains largely unsubstantiated and the level of comment carries little real conviction, its existence serves to underline the fact that working in the area of politics with Junior school children was, at every step, exploratory.

The method of exploration was an unpretentious one; it was a question of getting discussion started so as to see what would happen, particularly how the children themselves would control its directions and pace. What in fact did happen was that, time and again, a group would take off with an idea, extending and modifying it by individual contributions to a theme, as the following extract illustrates. Here the process is in the hands of eleven-year-olds asked for their views on learning about politics in school:

Janet: We should really learn about the government in one great subject about the world. All the things that happen, and the culture and the social life, and all things like that. The whole.

Jamie: We've got to vote. I mean, us children. We're not allowed to vote until we're eighteen, the government said that. But I think we should have more say – in the Common Market and things. We might make the wrong suggestions, but at least we've tried to be more mature in our ways.

Janet had previously made this point: People, about ten and over, should be able to vote. They're being more mature and they can discuss things like we're discussing things now.

I asked them: 'Do you think, then, that there should be something like a children's vote? Or should you have an adult vote?'

Janet: Yes, I think we should. Each family discusses it with their parents first, and then the parents give in the vote that we've all settled at together. Not just the parents saying: 'Right, I'm voting for the Conservatives, right, that goes in', I think they should all discuss it with the children first. Because the children might not want that when they're a bit older.

Jamie: I think it should be a separate children's vote, not a family, because they'd all have different views about it, and what would they vote then? It should be a separate vote, all the children with different votes. And whoever got in would get so many seats from the children. And adults the same.

Marcus: What would be a good idea would be if we had children in the Cabinet. Just a couple. They could face them with their views about education!

This conversation illustrates a considerable achievement on the children's part, not only in politics but involving what Janet described as 'the whole'. She was right, initially, to treat the question of learning about politics in school as part of a wider discussion about the nature of the curriculum generally, and she tried to deal constructively with the question that she, in her turn, had raised: of what education should be and should seek to do for children at that stage. I shall take her theme as a starting-point in a later chapter and try to develop it there.

The children's achievement as a group lies in their ability to use a political frame of reference convincingly. Their ideas about complex issues, while by no means fully developed, are usable, enabling them not only to make sense of the world as it is, politically, but to go a stage further and suggest alternative arrangements. And however original and startling these might appear, they are supported by relevant and logical argument. Their attempt to argue for voting on the grounds of sufficient maturity has one fascinating side-effect: it must surely make us wonder what any claim to political 'maturity' might rest upon.

Working with theories interested the older children, who frequently were able to handle ideas that were technically 'abstract', as early as nine. The existence of such a developing ability contradicts much in our present assumptions about what nine-year-olds, and even eleven-year-olds can do, and consequently of what we expect of them in educational settings. So there is a question to be asked: are we seriously underestimating our children at the most important stage in their education? If we are in fact ignoring, educationally, a developing capacity for rational thinking, then we might decide at some stage to raise the further question of what should be done to accommodate it. My argument is for the recognition and understanding of an ability apparent by eleven, and sometimes by nine years of age, but rooted in, and developing from, earlier achievements. And so we start by listening to what the seven-year-olds have to say, before going on to take into account what happens, year by year, in children's thinking, between that age and eleven.

THE SEVEN-YEAR-OLDS: FACT, FANTASY AND
ANTI-HEROES

At a school in Essex, two little girls, Pip and Sarah, took the same starting point that broke the ice successfully with all groups; it consisted of my producing a set of newspaper pictures of the current political leaders, for them to identify. Shown an incomplete set and asked who was missing, Pip easily made the connection, and was able to elaborate:

Pip: He's like the team leader of the Liberals. They are in sort of parties and they have leaders.

Question: What's a party?

Pip: When they all get together and do things.

Q: What kind of things do they do?

Pip: They talk about laws.

Q: Do they talk about laws and agree about everything, do you think?

Pip: Not everything, some things.

Sarah: A good law, and things like that.

Q: How do you know if a law is a good law?

Sarah: Well, because it would help people.

Q: What kind of ways would a law help people?

Pip: Sometimes when they put prices down it would help.

Sarah: They have to make sure that people in factories and things like that don't have to work too hard.

Q: Would you think a Prime Minister does all this by himself or do you think somebody helps him?

Sarah: Somebody helps him because all the parties help him.

Q: How does the Prime Minister decide who's going to help him?

Sarah: Because, when people vote for him, say he got three hundred, he will have three hundred people helping him to do all the rules.

Q: If you wanted three hundred people to help you, would you ask them all at the same time?

Sarah: I would just ask them all. Not just one at a time, about five, the good ones that do things all together.

Q: When someone gets to be Prime Minister, how do we know if he's a good Prime Minister?

Pip: Because you've got to let him make one rule, and see if he does a good rule. And if he don't do it properly, then they would know.

Q: What kind of things do you think a bad Prime Minister would do?

Sarah: If they kept all the prices high and things like that. And making things so no-one could play on them.

Q: What do you think should happen to a bad Prime Minister?

Sarah: He would get voted out.

Q: Pip?

Pip: I feel that if he was a bad Prime Minister no-one would like him, and they wouldn't do nothing that he says. Like Sarah says, vote him out because nobody wants a bad Prime Minister, because everybody wants the world to be nice.

Sarah: My grandfather, he wanted the Conservatives to win.

Q: Does he ever say why?

Sarah: No.

Pip: When we were on holiday, (naming a politician) he came on the beach on a hovercraft.

Q: Did you like him?

Pip: No, I thought he was horrible.

Q: Why?

Pip: Well, he keeps saying where he's going, and he does it like he's always the leader in all the world.

Q: And you don't like that?

Pip: No.

The volunteering of information, occurring above, is one of the ways children use to assert a stronger role in a discussion. They bring a gift to it, with all the implications of that gesture.

Q: Are you interested in things like who wins the election, and who's the Prime Minister?

Pip: My Mum and Dad aren't, but I am.

Q: I wonder why you are, if your Mum and Dad aren't?

Pip: I don't know – because they are always doing other jobs. They don't watch the telly. Most of the time they don't know what's going on.

Q: Do you ever tell them what is going on?

Pip: Sometimes, because when they are in the garden I watch the telly, the news and things like that, and see what is happening.

Q: Pip, who runs the country?

Pip: The Prime Minister. No, the Queen.

Q: Who is in charge?

Sarah: The Queen's in charge over him.

Q: Do you agree with that, Pip?

Pip: Yes. I think the Queen looks after all the country.

Sarah: Not just all the counties, all the country.

Q: Does the Queen do any work?

Pip: She visits people and writes things down on papers, and things like that.

Sarah: She visits other countries and she signs things, and she's very busy.

Q: What things does she sign?

Sarah: I don't really know.

Q: Does she make laws?

Pip: Well, does she have the power to make the laws?

Q: You don't think she makes them herself?

Pip: No, it's people like the Prime Minister.

Q: Does he tell people what to do?

Sarah: He makes the rules and tells people what to do. But if he keeps telling people to do naughty things, well then, no one would do as he would say.

Q: So we could please ourselves whether we did what he told us or not?

Sarah: Well, if he was a good Prime Minister and everybody liked him, they would.

These little girls found no difficulty in joining in a political discussion. At ease and interested, they were able to show some awareness of highly complex issues, for example of the limitations of power, of government by consent of the governed and the underpinning notion of accountability. In the absence of anything very much in the way of information about government, they can only guess about its organisation. But the guesswork is intelligent and there is an attempt to apply what is known and to make inferences, as Sarah did on the subject of what a 'bad Prime Minister' would do. She knew without having to think about it that high prices are an issue – this is rote-learning in social terms for today's children – but she tried to handle the concept and think about what other applications it could have. 'Making things so no one could play on them' is her thoughtful example of a deliberate misuse of Prime-Ministerial power. That her attempt to go beyond the stock 'prices' answer led her back to the egocentric concerns of childhood is typical – and inevitable – at her stage; what is impressive is her 'thinking through' of the question on her own terms.

Pip's countering of the question of whether the Queen makes the laws is also interesting. It seems to be an intuitive leap, bringing together the notion of laws and the concept of legitimate power for the first time. Her question indicates a 'readiness', in an educational sense, for further learning here. If this were so, if, during this kind of discussion, children's reflections bring them to a further stage in understanding, then the activity might well be considered justifiable in educational, as well as in research terms. So it seems reasonable to conclude that there are implicit questions raised here, concerning the whole concept of political education for children.

Jo, Wendy, Michael and Alan, seven-year-olds from South London, formed a different kind of discussion group, producing a set of individual performances, and the boys quickly embarked on a discussion of what a Prime Minister does. There was some perception of law-making, attached to the roles of Prime Minister and Queen, but confusion when more than a simple descriptive phrase was asked for. They were quite clear about the function of laws – to restrain people from the kind of activities they were familiar with from the media:

Alan: I read about it in the paper where a man was banned from driving because he had alcohol in his blood. From driving for a year!

Q: There should be laws about that, shouldn't there?

Michael: There is! And don't steal cars and don't do robberies and bank robberies and Pow-Pow and Boom-Booms like in America … in United States of America!

His style of communicating here seems to start from identifying with the action and trying to re-create it for the listeners. What appeared to have happened was that the children had absorbed such pieces of information as were readily available and made some intuitive connections between them. This is not to say they were at the mercy of anything and everything, completely vulnerable to suggestion. Leading questions, inserted to assess their disposition to agree with untested statements, were usually rejected, and the fact that this was not acceptable raises the further question of what sources of political information are regarded as valid. In any such list it seems that the media, especially television, will hold a dominant position.

Television was regarded as the basic political arena, in which the onus was on individuals to establish their credibility. Exactly how this was to be done was never formally established by the seven-year-olds as it was by some older groups who were able to work out criteria. The seven-year-olds, encountering individual politicians for the first time as television performers or personalities, and therefore encountering only a verbal performance, examined that performance critically. In fact this turned out to be an area of some interest and involvement for the children, especially on the subject of a politician's ability to communicate. Where Pip had taken a dislike to what one man had to say and his style of saying it, the two boys criticised another for what they took to be his refusal to communicate anything.

Michael: He signs things – Vote for Me! And some people wrote he's rotten and that gave me the idea. And when I saw him on TV – ugh – he's rotten!

Q: Just because you don't like the way he talks on television?

Alan: No, because (of) the way he talks about things.

Q: What do you mean, the way he talks about things?

Alan: Well, he – say you were asked a question, like 'What's the highest mountain in the world?' And you'd go: 'Er, I don't know, er, yeah, that, er. I don't know.' Like that. That's what he talks like.

Q: Do you mean he doesn't answer the question?

Alan: No, he does answer the question – well, not properly. I can't explain it, but as I said before, he doesn't answer it properly. He could say 'Mount Everest' and he could say other things about it, but he doesn't answer it properly!

The child had a struggle to communicate his meaning, but his strategy of using a clear, simple example worked.

   Different approaches between boys and girls were in evidence when it came to the question of identifying a good Prime Minister. The following exchange illustrates the interaction between the children in this group, and the varying amount of input from individuals that became established early in the situation:

Q: Wendy first. How would we know if he was a good Prime Minister?

(Silence from Wendy.)

Q: Don't you think we would know?

Wendy: I don't know.

Q: Do you know, Jo?

Jo: Yes. We might see him on TV.

Michael: I know what I'd do with him. Make him jump out of a hundred foot plane!

Q: But that's not what Prime Ministers are supposed to do, is it?

Michael: Yes it is! Just to test him to see if he's afraid or not. If he isn't afraid – without a parachute, that is – if he isn't afraid, he's a good Prime Minister!

Q: But if he jumped out of a plane a hundred feet high without a parachute, he wouldn't be a good Prime Minister very long, would he, because he'd be dead?

Michael: No, No, No. He'd have a couple of thousand mattresses ready on the floor – air-filled!

Q: Are you saying you only want somebody who's really brave and tough, and that's a good Prime Minister?

Michael and Alan: Yes.

There is a certain logic in the fantasy, struggling through the early childhood symbolism, but it is a highly personal mixture. Alan's thinking was already based in the real world, and the story for its own sake had little appeal, while the girls were not really able to deal with the question, for Jo's 'We might see him on TV' had been an evasion. Michael's account seems to owe something to television. Is there any more to it, we might ask, than this? Notions of leadership are conceptually linked with notions of authority, and here is the tacit awareness of the difference between formal and actual authority. Possibly gained in school, this awareness is projected on to the outside world as a need for, and belief in, the 'hero' as leader, one whose actual authority is a personal attribute, derived from the charisma of super-performance. It is worth remembering that such symbolic thinking can also be seen in adult political choices, apparently based on the assumption shared, and illuminated by, seven-year-old thinking here: that of the easy transfer of other kinds of ability into politics.

Perceptions of the Queen's role and activities differed between the two groups of children; differences existed even between the two pairs of little girls, and between the girls and boys. Pip and Sarah had the most developed concepts of the Queen's functions, and when questioned were able to decide which of their ideas to discard. These girls were able to present a fairly developed conceptual framework compared with the two others, whose information was scrappy. Here Wendy is anxious, expressing insecure answers as questions, while Jo seems to be recalling images:

Q: What does the Queen do, Wendy?

Wendy: Writes letters?

Q: What about?

Wendy: Sometimes when they're a hundred?

She was able to present only one idea, uncertainly held, having no category for 'they'. Jo was able to contribute two further ideas:

Jo: Well, she helps people and she wears precious jewels.

The two attributes are not logically connected, and apart from a later echoed agreement with Alan's statement: 'She takes the taxes from us for the Prime Minister', this was the extent of her contribution here.

The boys behaved rather differently; several influences dominated their dialogue at different points. The general impression was of the activities of a Robin Hood on Maundy Thursday, and the use of quaint expressions such as 'the poor' or 'her riches' showed an assimilation of language outside the normal usage of school, peer group and home (presumably children's television programmes were the source).

Alan: She takes the taxes from us for the Prime Minister.

Q: Does she?

Michael: And who does she give them to? Does she keep them for herself and spend them? In her riches?

Alan: I think she spends them on buildings and roads and gives some to the people that work. I think she gives her managers some, and twelve pounds a year to the poor.

Several aspects of the children's development of political concepts are revealed by the conversations of these two groups of seven-year-olds, and by comparisons between them.

Different styles of questioning elicit different responses. The information-seeking questions that are to some extent 'closed' (that is, specific answers are required and to a large extent these can be correct or incorrect) discover the awareness of facts, and reveal established attitudes. A more 'open-ended' type of question is more likely, from this evidence, to enable a questioner to draw both a child's interpretation of political matters, and any ability to generate further meaning. Allowing children to discuss with one another on this level gives valuable information on cognitive styles, and also on the ways in which they use and understand principles of classification. Dialogue tends at this stage to be carried on by means of statements rather than justifications, examples rather than reference to issues, and the limitations of intuitive and pre-conceptual thought were revealed in the language used. This shows, for example, in the use of wide (and therefore vague) categories and of 'things like that' for the object of actions, where purposes are not grasped but certain activities are understood to take place. However, there was also an awareness of structure in government, of co-operative relationships and the accountability of political figures as well as a spontaneous criticism of style of communication in politics.

Different levels of self-confidence were apparent between the groups. Conversation in the mixed group was dominated by the boys, who were quickly involved in new areas of discussion with considerable self-confidence, while the girls in the group, unable to match this, opted out at an early stage. By contrast, the Essex girls possessed considerably more information and showed a readiness to express and extend ideas.

The limits of 'pre-operational' thinking show in the difficulties children had with mentally 'mapping' a sequence of actions and with understanding relationships. The difficulties over ascribing more or less power to the Queen or Prime Minister are examples of these limitations, which were also illustrated by the children's attitudes to the television speaker they talked about. Absolute attributes ('He's rotten!') were employed, not relational or proportional ones.

What I have tried to show in this section is, firstly, that seven-year-olds can be seen to have some cognitive contact with the political world, and secondly, that this achievement encompasses political information, awareness, and not least, interest. Their basic concepts seem to be those of role or function, of people having political aims and purposes, and some notions of what these might be. What comes across perhaps most strongly in these extracts is the sense the children seemed to have of political power being limited, consented to, and conditional upon results. Their critical attitudes towards individuals rested on certain expectations, already formed, of what a politician should be and should do. In other words, they had already tacitly accepted a measure of participation in the political system.

THE EIGHT-YEAR-OLDS: 'THE BRITISH ISLES IS BIGGER, AND BETTER THAN THE PRICES!'

It was presented not as a political slogan, nor as self-evident truth, but as an eight-year-old's considered conclusion to the debate as that age-group saw it. For the question they worked on, and which seems to underpin their responses to whatever else they were asked about in politics, was the fundamental one: does it all boil down to 'the prices'? Or not?

Erica and Lynne, at school in Essex, had a point of view:

Q: Erica, what was the election all about?

Erica: About food (prices) going up.

Q: Yes, that's one of the things, but what were they voting for? What was the point of it all?

Erica: Because we wanted food to go down; it was going up.

Q: Can you help us there, Lynne?

Lynne: To see who is Prime Minister. The old Prime Minister gets chucked out the back door and the new one moves in. That's what my teacher said.

Q: Why do we change our Prime Minister?

Lynne: 'cause other people aren't happy with the Prime Minister that already is Prime Minister.

Q: And so what happens?

Lynne: They have another election.

Q: How does the Prime Minister get to be the Prime Minister?

Lynne: They have a vote and he is the leader of the party.

Q: What's a party, Erica?

Erica: When people get together.

Q: What do they get together for?

Erica: To see if things (prices) go up or down.

Asked about what kind of things political parties might disagree about, she returned to prices:

Erica: Agree about things going up.

Q: Do you mean some people want prices to go up, and some people don't?

Erica: I want them to go down.

For these children, politics is about the economics of their real world, and neither of them appeared to have any great interest in, or loyalty towards, public figures. Most children of this age found some difficulty in differentiating between the activities of the Prime Minister and those of the Queen, and this appears to have been largely because they had no clear conception of the Queen's functions. While aware that she 'helps the country' in some way, on being questioned they tended to assume that all her activities would necessarily have that effect; the general effect that came to the children appeared to be that of a presiding maternal presence.

The eight-year-old boys I talked to in their Essex school seemed, by comparison with the two girls, to have a less secure contact with day-to-day events. They were largely operating on an 'intuitive' or guesswork level, while making an effort to direct their thinking towards politics and it was interesting to see how one boy, encouraged by questions, was able to make a start on working out why politics is concerned with 'Arabs' and 'oil'. In the following extract, thinking seems to move on to some extent, as the children in their different ways become more interested in the subject.

Oliver and Vince on 'How does a person get to be Prime Minister?':

Oliver: Well, he says what is it on telly, and gets lots of votes that he wants, and then the most votes, then he wins. He's the one who gets the most votes wins. In other words, he fights you know, for it.

Q: What does a Prime Minister do, Vince? What's he there for?

Vince: Taking charge of the country.

Q: How does he take charge of the country?

Vince: Writes letters to other people.

Q: What do you think the letters might be about?

(No answer.)

Q: Vince, what might a bad Prime Minister do? Suppose he was a real terror, a real baddie, what might he do then?

Vince: Put up signs saying 'Keep Britain messy!'

Q: Oliver, what should happen to a bad Prime Minister?

Oliver: They should send him away. Or chuck him out.

Q: Send him away? Where to?

Oliver: To prison.

Q: How long for?

Oliver: Five years.

Q: Five years?

Oliver: Well, that's how long they spend for a Prime Minister.

Q: In this country, at the moment, do you think, from your watching the news, that we've got any problems? Anything we need the Prime Minister to sort out?

Vince: In our country there's been something happen because they won't give us no oil.

Q: Who wouldn't give our country oil?

Vince: Would it be the Arabs?

Q: So do you think the Prime Minister's job might have something to do with sharing out oil?

Vince: Yes.

The boys are prepared to 'chuck out' or imprison a 'bad' Prime Minister, although it seems from their idea of 'bad' behaviour on his part that they find it difficult to accept such an idea and play it down. Aggressive qualities are approved; the Prime Minister must 'fight' for his office. For them, he must be a positive leadership figure, although they are by no means certain of the exact channels for these qualities.

The 'mixed' eight-year-olds from South London presented a rather different situation. Here was interaction combined with strongly personal approaches to problems, and some interest in winning arguments. Plunging in at the start, Adrian attempted to give an account of the stages in becoming Prime Minister:

Adrian: Have to be quite clever - to be an MP and, to be an MP you have to go through a sort of thing – rules your life – and you have to run, and things like that.

This sequence was, however, incomplete at the final stage from lack of information, so lapsed into the symbolic structure of 'and things like that'. And Bob's symbolic thinking was evident in his phrasing, when a 'good Prime Minister' was seen as one who would 'let the Common Market go down, or if he's not a good Prime Minister he would let the Common Market go up'. This was extended by the explanation that he meant 'make the food prices go up' and that being a 'good Prime Minister' was related to controlling prices. Adrian had a more specific definition which he refused to weaken into a concern with prices, dealing instead with the larger issue:

Adrian: I think he should be a good Prime Minister because he'd be staying in the Common Market.

This choice from alternatives implies judgement but its content is limited, the premise seen as self-evident and self-justifying. Gina's perception of a 'good Prime Minister' was complex, generalised and tending strongly to the inoffensive:

Gina: Well, he should have imagination and he should be nice and talk to you.

The idea of a Prime Minister 'having imagination' was acceptable to the group. Gina's idea was validated, although its content was not examined for possible meaning until Adrian produced an interpretation:

Adrian: He'd be writing books!

And he defended this under Gina's gentle attack ('That would be funny!') by producing a categorical statement:

Adrian: Prime Ministers write books!

This is now presented as normal Prime Ministerial activity. But Gina was able to defend her objection:

Gina: What if he works? (Writing books is not work.) If he did, it would be funny!

For Gina, a 'bad Prime Minister' 'wouldn't be friendly and he wouldn't talk to you'. And Adrian, summarising the required qualities and accepting the premises of the other children, nevertheless clung to his own point of view.

Adrian: He'd let all the prices go up – then – if he'd talk to you, he wouldn't be friendly – and – he wouldn't write books!

Bob was now ready to present his own argument for Britain's being in the Common Market, opposition to which defined a 'bad' Prime Minister:

Bob: He wouldn't stay in the Common Market ... So if we had – a shortage of salt – we wouldn't be able to help, we wouldn't be able to do it by ourselves. We'd need help from other countries. If we wouldn't be in the Common Market, we wouldn't get that salt, ourselves.

Not yet ready for dealing with issues as abstractions, he is yet able to approach principles through using a concrete example. And motivation counts. He is sufficiently motivated towards solving this problem to construct the technique for dealing with it.

Gina's insistence on a 'friendly' Prime Minister reveals her undeveloped ability to categorise – either to recognise a 'set' of qualities that make a Prime Minister good as a Prime Minister – the role attributes or to separate ideas of a distant public figure from her experience of immediate relationships. Hers is, to some extent, the 'benevolent leader' image of childhood, which appears to be less prevalent in our own political system than in some others. In choosing the 'friendly' image, she was not able to consider what the opportunities for such interaction might be, or its terms. And whether she was referring to personal encounters or a style of communication via television, is not really clear, although her phrasing indicates an expectation of personal contact. Understanding of the question appears to be incomplete and there is a consequent re-interpretation of it, hinging on Gina's restricted use of 'good'. (She provides an interesting link with the kind of difficulties children often have in dealing with early mathematical concepts in Piagetian terms, when they answer a question *as they understand it*, on the basis of limited concepts. This provides, not 'wrong' answers as such, but valuable information for teaching purposes.)

Bob revealed a different kind of confusion in his answers to consecutive questions:

Q: Who did you want to win the by-election? Do you remember?

Bob: Mr Wilson.

Q: Do you mean you wanted the Labour Party to win? If there was an election tomorrow, which party would you want to win?

Bob: Liberal.

Harold Wilson had not in fact been a candidate in the by-election, so Bob was speaking in a symbolic sense, to signify the party he would have chosen at that point in time, although holding a different preference on the question of a future election. Reasons for affiliation were not yet accessible, for in spite of unanimous Liberal support, none of the children was able to explain it. Bob produced a personality-preference basis:

Q: Has liking a party got to do with liking the person who leads it, or is that something else?

Bob: It's the same. I would say it's because I like the person.

Neither little girl was able at this stage to construct a perception of aims or purposes in politics. Bob's construction was economic. Politics was about the 'money situation'; it was also about the 'price situation', which appeared to display an analytic ability not shared by at least one other member of the group, for Adrian was not able to accept this:

Adrian: That's the same as the money situation!

The particular phrasing used reveals the influence of the media. Adrian's ability to identify one problem led him to search for explanation which, however, eluded him at this stage in his thinking:

Adrian: We're running out of money, because the people who are printing the money – they think – we might as well not make some, because we've made such a lot as it is. Nowadays, people are losing quite a lot of money.

The child's attempt at explanation is interesting on two counts: firstly because in making it he was spontaneously extending the range of his thinking. As the lapse into fantasy indicates no previous correction made for him, a first attempt can be assumed here. Secondly, this appears to be an attempt to validate a particular idea by presenting it for comment. Bob's economic ideas were presented succinctly, not to say ominously:

Bob: ... There isn't much money in Britain and prices are going up.

Neither boy used the term 'inflation', the nearest attempt being Bob's 'rise'. The word generated an illustrative example from Gina who applied it to wages rather than prices, but shifted her uncertainly-held ground at once, under correction from Adrian:

Gina: When the miners – they wanted one thousand pounds for their work – for their wages.

Adrian: It's a hundred pounds!

Gina: Oh, yes, a hundred pounds, yes!

The question 'Have we got any other problems?' produced successful, if somewhat pessimistic responses from three of the children:

Bob: There's lot of people on strike.

Adrian: Petrol's going up ... and now, it's about two pounds ... They put it up. I think it's about seven – I think it's about five pounds for four gallons now!

Marian: And food is getting short!

On being asked about the Queen's activities, the girls produced different ideas and images from the boys, which perhaps resulted from different constructions of the word 'work'.

Q: Gina, what do you think the Queen does all the time?

Gina: She sits around, and ... sometimes she goes out to a party.

Q: Anything else? Do you think she does any work?

Gina: No.

Q: Do you, Marian?

Marian: She has servants.

Q: Any different kind of work?

Marian: Yes.

Q: What kind of work does she do, do you think?

No response.

There was unanimous agreement that the Queen 'is more important than the Prime Minister' and an ability to find terms on which to justify this conviction.

Marian: Oh, because the Queen sort of looks after the country.

Bob: Because the Queen lives in a better place than the Prime Minister because she's ... better than him ... and she's ...

Gina: (Prompting) In charge of the others!

Bob and Gina successfully matched concepts here, agreeing: 'She's in charge of the British Isles'.

Q: And the Prime Minister isn't?

Bob and Gina: No.

Q: What is he in charge of, then?

Bob: He's in charge of the agreement market.

Gina: And he's in charge of all the prices.

Q: What's the difference between being in charge of the British Isles and being in charge of all the prices?

Gina: The difference is the British Isles is bigger, and better than the prices.

This statement appeared to mark a stage in conceptual progress for Gina. She had related two sets of activities, regarding one as dominant over the other. Whether she was able to regard 'the prices' as a sub-set of activities implicit in 'the British Isles' is not completely clear, but both generalised and specific aspects of power and control had emerged conceptually. This achievement at this point in time may well have been due to the successful validation of some of her concepts with Bob's help, resulting in increased confidence in her own judgement. Adrian once more attempted a summing-up:

Adrian: The Queen looks after nearly the whole country – all the countries in the world, compared with the Prime Minister who just looks after England and tries – thinking whether England should stay in the Common Market.

Q: You think the Queen looks after all the countries in the world?

Adrian: The Queen, she mostly travels, and while the Prime Minister, he doesn't travel very much, he usually stays in England quite a lot of the time.

He had succeeded here in producing criteria for judging the issue. Categories of activities were established on the basis of what was known. With more knowledge of the political system and observation of daily events his ability to categorise can be expected to keep pace with that experience. For the time being, he had done as much as he could with the information and experiences available. This is also true of the other children grasping, at eight, the political issue nearest their own reality – 'the prices' and edging steadily towards the splendid self-confidence of nine years old, that marks the 'take-off' stage in thinking about politics. Thinking which seems, even at eight, to be about more than just 'the prices'.

THE NINE-YEAR-OLDS: WORKING WITH IDEAS

Alan, Jo and Wendy were brought together again, nearly two years later as nine-year-olds. Michael had left the school by this time, and there were two newcomers to the group, Peter and Martin.

Q: Can anyone tell me what the Prime Minister does?

Alan: He decides where the tax goes.

Q: What are taxes about?

Alan: You have to pay so much per pound to the government so they can have money for public services and things like that.

Q: What do you think a good Prime Minister would be like?

Alan: Like the one we've got now.

Q: Do you think Mrs Thatcher would make a good Prime Minister?

Martin: I think she would. I don't know why, but I think she would.

Alan: I don't.

Q: Why not?

Alan: She's a woman!

There was general laughter at this forthrightness, and Jo immediately took up the theme:

Jo: She'd make all the men do the work!

Q: Do you think that's not a job for a woman?

Jo: No, but say she's still got a home and some children, she would have to come running to one place and then go back home!

Q: Suppose she didn't have any children. Do you think that just because she's a woman she couldn't do it?

Jo: Yes.

Q: What about Wendy?

Wendy: I don't know.

Q: Haven't you thought about it?

Jo: I've never thought about a lady Prime Minister – never!

Q: I wonder why?

Jo: I don't think they are just like the men Prime Ministers.

Q: Is it because they are better?

Jo: No.

Q: Is there anything about the Prime Minister's job you don't think a woman could do?

Martin: One woman made a Prime Minister. I can't remember her name. She's got strange white hair, white there and black there (indicating by a gesture on his own hair), I can't remember what country, either.

Q: India, is it?

Martin: India, that's it.

Q: Do you remember her name now?

Martin: No I can't. I can't remember.

Q: Do you know what I mean when I say 'politics'?. Can you tell me what politics is about?

Peter: About the government, the work of the government.

Martin: The work of the country, where the people try to make it much better, that live there.

Q: What do you think, Alan?

Alan: What everybody else says.

Q: Tell me what you think?

Alan: Well, some politicians are better than others.

Q: Better than others?

Alan: James Callaghan, he's better from ... better Prime Minister than Michael Foot.

Q: Why?

Alan: Well, it's just that Michael Foot would have ideas that you would not be able to choose what school you would like to go to, and things like that. Almost communist.

Q: Do you know what communist means?

Alan: Yes. If you do something, break the law, you do not get a fair trial. You just get chucked into prison.

(Laughter from the group at this.)

Q: Do the rest of you think he is right about that?

Martin: Yes, I think so.

Q: Is this country a communist country?

All: No!

Q: Do you think we are freer in this country than in some others, or not so free? Do we have more rules or less rules?

Martin: We have more rules, more than in some countries.

This was generally agreed, and seen as a desirable state of affairs. Spontaneously, the children began to make comparisons:

Martin: We are better off in this country than they are in other countries, although there's more space in the other countries.

Peter: Some countries haven't got many houses or big buildings.

Jo: You see people dead on the TV. Some people sort of bleeding to death – starving – in the deserts or something.

Alan: You see people just tied up in sacks, that have been killed.

All of this was seen as relevant, and proportionate to, the rule of law. The difference between a law and a rule was understood well enough for explanation in which the children pointed out the difference between the rules of their school and the laws of the land. Universalising these became a moral problem for Jo and when her position was challenged by Alan's logic the two children developed a dialogue that took off to a new level of argument, working with two different concepts of rights:

Jo: I don't know why the Prime Minister doesn't do something about it.

Q: Our Prime Minister?

Jo: Mm.

Q: Do you think he could?

Jo: If he tried, yes.

Q: What kind of things do you think he might do?

Alan: He can't do anything in foreign affairs. He can't stop the stuff that the Spanish are doing. I've seen – I've heard reports about that.

Jo: I mean ... say there are some people dying?

Q: So – Alan tells that our Prime Minister can't do things in other countries?

Alan: He can't because he has no right to interfere with their affairs.

Q: You said the PM hasn't got a right to interfere. What is it to have a right?

Alan: It's to have a permission to go – to do something which other people can't do.

Jo: In other countries, perhaps they've got some other Prime Ministers of their own, but they don't help?

Q: So, if those Prime Ministers don't help, you think that our Prime Minister should?

Jo: Yes, yes. At least they'll get some money, if they're running out!

Q: And Alan's telling us that he can't because he hasn't got any right to do so?

Alan: He hasn't, because, if the countries don't belong to Britain, they have their right to go their own way, and do what they want. And their government has to do what concerns their country.

Jo: Well, look; what about if they're dying, then the Prime Minister is away, or something, looking in other countries, to see what happens in other countries?

Alan: He still doesn't have a right, because they don't belong to us. He just doesn't have a right to interfere with any things that happen in other countries. It's their country, they can go their own way and do what they want.

Jo: What about if the nurses, and doctors, in the other countries, are dying as well? What happens?

Alan: Well then they'll appeal for help, like when there was that civil war in the Lebanon. The side that was fighting once appealed for help from another country, and then the side appealed for help here, and we gave them help by collecting stamps and sending them in to *Blue Peter*. You should have seen all the stuff they got for it!

Jo: Well, I thought you just said that foreign people should do it, didn't you? So why doesn't the Prime Minister, our Prime Minister, do it?

Alan: Because they haven't, they haven't called to him for help.

At seven, Jo had been unable to match the boys' willingness to talk and to explore ideas; by nine, an obvious change had taken place, to the extent that she was ready to produce and defend a proposition in politics. Alan had also progressed, from using a seven-year-old's mixture of fact, fantasy and practical criticism to dealing, at nine, with factual information and using it to show some understanding of issues. Both children, at nine, were able to hold a logical exchange on a political problem and to expand the discussion when another child introduced fresh material:

Martin: I've got a point with Jo there. We have got missionaries out in Uganda, for people that aren't very well and they are helping them.

Jo: They are risking their lives to go down there and try to help!

Alan: Yes, but they are making people better and making farms to grow food so that they can be fit and well to teach them the Bible. So that in a way is just because they want to teach them the Bible. Besides, that's an underdeveloped country. In some places of the world people are still eating humans. But here are we spending millions of pounds shooting rockets up to the moon, to Jupiter and Mars and Venus. So that's an underdeveloped country – a country that hasn't got much technology.

Jo: What good would it do, sending people up into the air and on to Mars and Venus?

Peter: To learn things. To learn things about the atmosphere.

Q: Is that as important as feeding people?

All: No.

Martin: It might be.

Alan: Because if we send rockets up to discover if there's life on other planets, if we find intelligent life like we are, then they could be in trouble with their food. So if we leave off a couple of million pounds for people down here we might save hundreds of lives up on other planets.

The construction of argument, defending of positions and extending of categories that is apparent during this conversation as the children drew responses from each other, illustrates their growing ability to work with ideas. Similarly, other groups developed fresh ideas.

Two other groups of nine-year-old children were involved: Susannah and Margaret, at school in urban industrial Essex; and, in South-East London, Marcus, Sally, Janet and Jamie. In conversation these nine-year-olds also showed developmental differences from earlier stages. Political terminology was used easily and the discussion of political actions and situations took place critically, with some feelings of involvement. Information in response to questions tended to present reasons and explanations and there was a noticeable quickening of the pace of discussion. Asked to describe a 'good Prime Minister', Margaret and Susannah explained the situation:

Margaret: They have a sort of list, you see, and they have to answer questions, and that. And they see all their brains.

Q: Do you mean before a party chooses who's going to be Prime Minister?

Margaret: Yes.

Q: Supposing a man's got to be Prime Minister – you know, he's there, he's working. How would we know if he's a good Prime Minister?

Susannah: Well, he pays good prices and puts up wages and then he puts down food prices.

Q: Anything else?

Susannah: Well, he looks after the country well, and you give him about half a year to see if he's done any good for you.

Q: What kind of things do you have to do to look after the country well?

Susannah: Well, we would have to make him give us more wages, and if, like my Mum's having a baby, and she had to go in (hospital), and my Dad had to be off work, well I think he gets about eight pounds a week – so it's really hard to look after us. Well, what I reckon, they should give up more, what a Prime Minister should do, he should give the men more money to live to pay for rent, and tax, and we get ever so much tax to pay, but I reckon we shouldn't get so much tax.

Q: Margaret, how would we know if a man wasn't a good Prime Minister?

Margaret: Each person would get less money.

Q: What should happen to him if he is a bad Prime Minister?

Margaret: Get the sack.

Q: Susannah. Do you agree with that?

Susannah: No, I think he should be made to resign himself.

Q: What is the difference between getting the sack and being made to resign?

Susannah: Well, you can't really sack a Prime Minister because people have got to say 'We want an election' or something like that, and the person has got to agree. And if at work you get the sack it's not quite like a Prime Minister.

Q: Margaret, are you going to argue that one with her? You can't sack a Prime Minister?

Margaret: It depends. You can sack a PM, but when the next Labour and things come, the person who gets the highest amount of it can come to be the next Prime Minister.

Q: He might get re-elected anyway? You might get him back?

Margaret: Yes.

Susannah showed that she found the economic sphere of political activity unsatisfactory without some underpinning philosophies, and began spontaneously to develop a theme of her own:

Susannah: I think that this world should really ... well, you shouldn't bother about money, you should share everything. If, no, what I mean, down our church there's a tramp and he's been living there for a long time. Well, I feel very sorry for him because when the Boys' Brigade go there they throw lots of stones at him. I think people, educational people, should give him a home which is nice and warm and he should have plenty of food and I think it's ridiculous to pay money for tax. I think we should share everything, money and everything.

Q: Don't you think paying taxes is a way of sharing?

Susannah: Oh, yes, it is really but, well, if, you can't give a person too much tax because once my Dad was given a lot of tax to pay and he didn't have the money. You can't have too much out of the people because if you ask them for some amount of money and they haven't got it they aren't going to have food, a home or anything. They have to start selling things. The poor people shouldn't have to pay tax. The people who haven't got any children should pay the most of the tax.

Q: Why is that?

Susannah: Because the people with – the old age pensioners haven't got much money because the people have retired and the people with children have got to pay it all out their wage for their children and all the food – but the other people, all they have got to do is pay the money for them and their wife.

Asked about acceptable ways of changing existing laws, she was quite ready to accept the implications of her definition of social justice, and to acknowledge the conflicts in a pluralist society:

Susannah: The thing is that so many people want different laws so it's going to be quite a fight in this country from now on, because, well, there's little amounts of one party and there's little amounts of the other, and if them parties get together there's going to be lots of fights.

Susannah's exposition was accepted by Margaret, who tried to solve the social problem by applying a separatist philosophy:

Q: Do you agree with that, Margaret? So many people wanting so many different things?

Margaret: Yes, I should think what they should do ... live in groups and things like that.

Q: You mean live separately?

Margaret: Yes.

Susannah: I think people, that they shouldn't always live separately – like if me and my friend have an argument and say 'Ooh, you've got fleas, I don't like you' – well, this is how grown-ups, adults, act sometimes – but I think it's stupid, fighting and all that. We should all be friends and lend each other things and we should all have a nice cosy house with a fire and bed and that, and well really, why has money got to get in it? Why do we really need money? If people got together, all the world, or just Britain, got together, they should really, money should be taken out of the world and then they can make us just live without paying anything and there should be provided, no, we should just pick up from the land what we want. It's like a farm, they have to do their own thing. Well, we can pick out our own things excepting if it's in a different country they can lend us some like there's something from every country isn't there? We've got coal.

Q: Yes, I can see that point of view. Do you think that when you grow up you might want to be a Member of Parliament?

Susannah: No, I'd like to live in the countryside. I wouldn't like to actually get in these rough fights and that – I'd just let them get on with it and live my own way. But I would be concerned about it but I'd just keep out the way and let them carry on – if they want to be silly, they can be silly.

Q: So you don't want to be the Prime Minister then and make everybody live like that?

Susannah: No, but the thing is if people would listen to it – first of all you have got to get people to listen. Some people don't – they just go around madly and do things wrong. Some people, it's like forest fires, some people mean to do it – they do it deliberately. Some people just want to live an easy life, like, most of the families in Britain or the other countries, they want to live an easy life.

Susannah saw social conflict as both temporary and capable of being resolved, which became a moral imperative for her. The question of justification was neatly turned on analogy, as her argument on the necessity of 'being friends' swung from individuals to group and collective situations. Ultimately, it was the refusal of friendship and goodwill that had to be justified. Margaret, on the other hand, accepts this as a fact of life, to be accommodated, and so the two little girls are working with quite different, conflicting views on human nature here:

Margaret: Some people should stay friends, like all the others (who do), like Susannah and I, we are best friends. They should stay friends like that so they can all get together. But you can't do this, because all they do is argue.

Q: Did you mean that, Susannah?

Susannah: No. Well if they get together they will fight, but ... I think they should all become friends and live happily together and not fight like anything. It's like down our street, there's lots of fights down there, but me and my next-door neighbour are very good friends, and some people are. They are very good friends to each other. If, like, my nanny wanted something left in our freezer, well, we let her and if she's run out of milk we lend her a pint of milk but she gives it to us back. So why can't they just be friends?

Susannah's refusal to accept a Hobbesian view of human nature led her to reject Margaret's alternative and, with all the instincts of a demagogue, appeal to higher principles in what turned out to be a fairly emotional speech. In the mode of classical political philosophers, she contrasted an account of human nature, not regarded as intractable, with a theory of the world as it could be. For the classic position, a theory of education is also required, and she reached for this: '... the thing is if people would listen to it – first of all you have got to get people to listen'. There appears to be an assumption here of a rational general will that needs only to 'listen' to find its own best interests. She saw the Queen in a crucial role here.

Susannah: I think the Queen herself should choose the Prime Minister – and us, of course – but I think she really should convince the people. The trouble is the Queen is supposed to help us – she is helping us in a lot of ways now, but ...

It seemed that during this interview both little girls consolidated some of their notions initially, eventually reaching a point where they were able to develop alternative social constructions. Susannah's emotional involvement enabled her to reach a stage of thinking and self-expression not usually associated with nine-year-olds and politics. The source of this interest was the home and the mass media, '... my Dad talks a lot to me about it and really I watch a lot of telly', but there appeared to be little doubt that she had developed her own conceptual framework and was not only building upon it, but prepared to hold and defend her ideas. How typical is Susannah's political thinking of the nine- to ten-year-olds?

The ability to consider the world as it is and to see alternative social solutions belongs to a further stage of thinking, according to Piaget. Susannah appears to have achieved this ability in a particular way; her examples from immediate surroundings are used as a mental pivot, enabling her to remain securely anchored in reality, while exploring the theoretical possibilities that interest her. She brings formal theory under control through exemplifying, and the next stage, for her, will be development of the ability to dispense with the need for this aid.

At nine, differences in quality of children's responses from those of the younger age-groups make both a quicker pace of discussion possible and a larger area of subject matter available. Responses demonstrate the children's willingness to be involved in political discussion and to carry the terms of it further than was initially asked of them.

One example of this can be seen in the remark of one of the girls on recognising a photograph, 'We *should* know him! Mr Wilson', which appears to accept a responsibility for collecting information. Her continuation, 'I've seen him on television and I want to do that again', states an intention of contributing further information and ideas to the discussion.

Marcus was well-informed, which was the point he wished to establish early in the proceedings, and was able to do so:

Q: How does a man get to be Prime Minister?

Marcus: Oh, first of all he becomes the leader of a party, and if they get – if in a general election they get a lot of people in their party who've been elected, that party wins, and the leader of that party becomes Prime Minister.

This boy produced a particular account of how he felt he had gained his knowledge about politics:

Marcus: My Dad ... tells me quite a lot about politics, for if I don't understand things. And – I think I was *born* with most of it, really!

Sally, also nine and well-informed, had a different explanation:

Sally: Well, I learn it mainly because Daddy's on a committee and we have meetings. But also, you see, I'm rather ixquisitive (for inquisitive) about it, and I keep on asking, and it gets on to very many things – explanations. And you find out why the government rules, and the Queen doesn't just do it all by herself, and things like that. And I think that's mainly why I know. And sometimes I listen to things on the news, and they have bits from things. Or sometimes I just listen to this programme ...

Janet was also interested enough, at nine, to learn from the media:

Janet: I find it out from the telly and the radio, that I mostly listen to when I come home from school. There's usually a political broadcast on, on the radio, and I usually listen to it, and Mummy explains it to me, and she tells me what it all means, and things like that. That's why.

The group's discussion on democracy stemmed from Sally's definition:

Sally: It (democracy) means that – well, it's not like a communist country where you have the people above everybody else saying exactly what it's going to do. The people are free to – do what they like –

and, just see – which, sort of, feeling what to do which comes out. And feel they want to do it!

Her emphasis on the affective aspect having gained unanimous support, some analysis of its principles was attempted:

Marcus: I think they (parties) must disagree on some things.

Q: Or there wouldn't be any point in having them, would there?

Marcus: No. We'd be able to govern ourselves, if they agreed with everything one person said ... If one man said 'Who agrees with this?' and everybody shot their hands up, in the Houses of Parliament, there'd be no use having a party, really. Just a few men.

Q: What's good about democracy?

Phil: Because you're free.

Q: Are you free to do anything you like, in a democracy?

Phil: No. There's some rules.

Q: What are the rules for? Are rules a good idea?

Phil: To keep – the work – Britain – going, and (so) it doesn't go wrong.

His faith in the rule of law was as yet undifferentiated into reasons for commitments, but not so Sally:

Sally: Well, we need it to keep the people in order, because if everybody did what they liked, we'd be rather a rotten country, and we wouldn't get anywhere, and money would just sort of be wasted, and – we'd end up living like sluts, you know – we just wouldn't be organised.

A characteristic of this group was the balance of discussion, which contributed very much to its pace; as topics changed, all the children's interests were able to re-focus on the new aspect of discussion. There were stronger members of the group in discussion but no persistent dominance by the boys, as had occurred in the younger mixed groups. On the contrary, these nine-year-olds showed considerable courtesy in debate; disagreement was rationalised, interruptions very few, and support enthusiastic, as in Marcus's agreement with Sally, 'She's put it – she's taken it all out of my mouth!'. The children listened to each other and this in itself reveals a developing capacity to consider other viewpoints and to accept the possibility of alternative solutions to particular problems, a capacity which is characteristic of the stage of formal operations or abstract thinking.

These conclusions support those already drawn from considering the earlier discussions with the Essex children: that the nine-year-old stage is a period of consolidation and expansion, of making connections between separate ideas that have already been acquired in some form. So as a result of more information having accumulated, more efficient interpretation of the political world becomes possible. Where this interpretation is insecure or illogical, it is often because the basic information is not available to children (for example, the precise nature of the Monarch's functions or the formal procedures of the passage of a bill through Parliament). There seems to be little justification for such factual information not being included in the Primary curriculum in schools at present.

Some children, as appears from their ability to interact in discussion, are developing by this age an ability for rational inquiry in political matters. This, it is suggested, is the distinctive achievement of the nine-year-old stage.

THE TEN-YEAR-OLDS: COMING TO TERMS WITH
THE WORLD OUT THERE

There were no Utopian constructs from these ten-year-olds, no ideal societies or attempts to pursue the form of justice. If some of the nine-year-olds gave us political philosophy on the grand scale that its founding fathers would have approved, the ten-year-olds are analysts of what is. The idea of fairness, that can be worked out and applied through knowledge of the facts of a situation, became a favourite theme that was used in widely differing ways by Nick and Roger, and Helen and Selina at school in Essex, and Pam, Toni, Ben and Chris in South London. We join the two boys, Nick and Roger, handling some basic political concepts with ease and interest, as Nick explains the necessity for political parties:

Nick: Because if some people get elected and they're not so good, people might want a change. But if they haven't got another political party they wouldn't be able to change, and they'd still have the same man to carry on for them.

Roger saw inter-party differences as useful and purposeful:

Roger: ... so that they can get some policies that they can put through Parliament.

We can see the political frame of reference strengthening here, his language indicating a network of concepts developing and becoming usable.

Nick: And it has to be approved by the Queen, and only then can it be made the law.

He was able to identify the general processes of law-making:

Q: If people want to change the law, could they?

Nick: No, not people, unless they could go to someone and tell them that this is their idea, and if the person likes it, and if he's an MP, he'd try and put it through Parliament.

On violence as a political method, the boys turned to discussing conflict in Ireland:

Q: Is there a better way?

Nick: Yes. If you go and talk to the people about why the army should be there. If you don't want them there, ask them to go and give them the reasons.

Q: Do you think that this is important, that people understand the reasons?

Nick: Yes!

Q: Do you think that if people do know the right reasons, then they would act on them?

Nick: Yes.

Q: Roger?

Roger: Yes!

Q: It's just a question of people understanding what the right reasons are?

Roger: Yes.

Their shared views on rationality were positive.

Helen thought a Prime Minister helped to make laws in the Houses of Parliament and Selina thought he had help with this, but was unable to specify from whom. Her 'good' Prime Minister would 'put the prices of food down instead of up', and Helen's would 'give people more wages', while the 'bad' Prime Minister would 'do all the opposites'. Deciding that a bad Prime Minsiter should be replaced:

Selina: They should get another man to vote for.

Q: How would we go about that?

Selina: Don't know.

The area of likeliest disagreement between the political parties was identified:

Selina: Some people think the food prices should go up and some people think they should go down, and some people think they should stay where they are.

Q: Which kind of people might think that food prices should go up, do you think?

Helen: People who run shops want more money.

This was the only unsuccessful interview, in that the girls were completely uninterested in the subject under discussion. There was neither involvement in issues, nor evidence of particular observation, and only minimal awareness of processes from the two. They were pleasant, polite, obviously not of less than average intelligence or abilities, but the subject for them was a boring one, and in discussion there was no spontaneous interaction, volunteering of information or opinion.

This conversation tells us something about the place of interest in the development of political concepts, and different levels in children's motivation. The eldest group, the two girls, had passed through the same experiences as the younger, in the school context. There was a difference in personality types between them and younger groups. Selina and Helen, close friends, were the quietest, most self-contained, apparently the most introvert pair interviewed. To say that they had passed through the same school situations does not, obviously, mean that they had had identical experiences, or assimilated the same concepts or information from shared experiences as other children. Neither of these girls was in the habit of watching television news programmes; neither was interested. Neither of them knew, or would guess at, what politics might be about, nor had ever voted for anything. This latter fact may be pertinent.

The girls had, at that stage, encountered only one issue which appeared to them of any real significance – the immediate one of food prices and this, as day to day events held little interest for them, seemed to be the only 'growth point' likely to expand. In terms of a political education curriculum, an awareness of prices changing could be a fruitful starting place for children, an interest for building on. Without the stimulus of this kind of programme at school, their political horizons may well never be wider.

Presenting political education to those whose initial response is limited will no doubt be one of the problems that will be faced, as curriculum change takes place. What can be learned from conversing with children like Helen and Selina is that innovation in this area may have a mixed reception. For some, apathy will have to be countered and motivation strategies devised. What can also be learned, by setting the discussion in the context of the discussions with all the children interviewed, is that the great majority of children involved showed positive and lively interest in talking about politics. Typical of this was the attitude of the London ten-year-olds. At the outset, Pam and Toni recognised Mrs Margaret Thatcher from a newspaper picture which showed only a fraction of her, in a crowd.

Q: How can you tell from a tiny bit of her?

Both girls: Her hair-style! The way her hair's done, and then there's the blue coat!

Q: How can you tell it's a blue coat from a newspaper?

Both girls: She always wears that coat!

Neither of the two boys, Chris and Ben, contributed to this, but as discussions developed among the four children, the basic interaction proved to be between the boys. Ben then neatly encapsulated the process of becoming Prime Minister:

Ben: Oh, well ... there's a number of parties and they have an election and all the people vote and the party that gets the most, then their leader, he's Prime Minister.

He thought this happened once a year, and perceived some mechanism for change, but he held this on a pre-conceptual level, not as a secure idea.

Ben: When the old Prime Minister ... when one of the Prime Ministers, he might start lacking – you know, not doing well. And they decide to change him.

Q: Who decides to change him?

Chris: Parties!

Q: Parties?

Chris: The House of Lords.

There was some perception of processes here, but of their existence rather than their form. Without sufficient information to work on there was a relapse into intuitive thinking and a loss of the logic of the process. A question about the characteristics of a good Prime Minister led to a consideration of qualities necessary for leadership. Toni's statement, 'Got to have faith in yourself', was in contrast to Chris's development of his first premise:

Chris: You've got to know that you've got ... co-operation with other people in the party.

Ben: (Interrupting – usefully, as it happened, as this provided Chris with the support he needed at this point.) Yes, you've got to be ... (failing to find a word).

Chris: You've got to have good co-operation with the managements – you know – Fords, and things like that.

Q: (To try to get him to persevere with working this out further.) Co-operation with the management. Why do you need to be a co-operative person?

Chris: If you ain't a co-op – co-op – co-operative person there'd be no agreement. You know, you'd have arguments and you won't be able to say, to tell them, anything.

This was an adequate early working out of accommodation of interests between groups.

The concept of democracy itself was not available to any member of the group and when they began to attempt some analysis, it was to break down the idea of the 'rule of the people' into particular examples of authority and responsibility.

Chris: Yes, people do some ruling ... they do ruling in management you know, in companies like the manager of the water boards, and ... the manager of a garage.

This provided, in its use of different applications, an illustration of Piaget's 'conservation' principle at work in political terms. For just as a child who has the 'conservation' principle well established knows that a measured amount of liquid does not change in quantity when poured into differently-shaped containers, even though it takes on different shapes and levels, and *looks* different, so a political application arises (for example, when a child understands that an abstract term retains what is distinctive in its meaning through a variety of differing circumstances).

A model of political relationships was then provided by co-operative effort:

Q: Have you any feelings about the Queen?

Toni: Sometimes.

Pam: Well, I haven't got any feelings about the Queen – but she isn't a person. She's a person but not an ordinary person like us – you know, she's high up.

Toni: A higher person than us.

Chris: I think ... little bits are left out, you know, lower bits.

Both Girls: Like a jigsaw!

Q: And which piece of the jigsaw would the Queen be?

Toni: High!

Chris: Oh, she'd be up high!

Pam: She'd probably be the frame! Yes, she'd be the frame. You make the frame first and then you collect them on to the frame to work, you know.

Q: If she was in a jigsaw, would she be the biggest person in the jigsaw?

Chris: No.

Q: Who would be?

Chris: God!

This building of a shared concept by adding constructively to another's suggested idea and using their imagery shows children moving on from purely egocentric thinking to accepting another person's viewpoint. It is a move towards freeing thought from dependence on subjective sense-data. The children in building this model, make an original variation on the familiar 'pyramid' construct of a hierarchy, and provide an example of group problem solving.

Supporting this group effort and making it possible, is a shared notion of formal authority, and its language. Invoking the ultimate authority 'God', Chris changed the terms of the discussion and ended its possibilities. Here, the children are already aware that you cannot mix two separate language-games. The particular use of the image of the jigsaw and the frame holds certain difficulties for interpretation. We might want to ask whether in this extract the children have regressed to symbolic thinking or conversely, if they have made a leap to much greater levels of sophistication in their use of analogy. As they are working to compare relationships, and neither inventing a story nor turning the situation into some form of play, the latter interpretation would seem to be more correct.

Party, as a focus for loyalty or even interest, was a non-starter. Margaret Thatcher's potential as Prime Minister, however, was a different matter.

Ben: I used to like Mr Heath, not Mrs Thatcher. Forgot all about Mr Heath, you know!

Q: I wonder why there haven't been any lady Prime Ministers before?

Ben had the question under conceptual control:

Ben: Oh, because they haven't been top of the party ... It depends on the party ... It does, depends on the party.

The question of what politics is about produced different reactions, Pam's choice of 'the Common Market' generating an argument on pros and cons and giving Chris a chance to polish his use of 'imports' and 'exports'.

Chris: We wouldn't get imports from other countries. We wouldn't be able to do business with other countries, and you know, get exports. We wouldn't be able to get money from them.

Q: Don't you think so?

Chris: No ... because, well, they don't give us imports – we don't pay them, we give them exports ... they don't pay us.

Ben's first choice of political subject matter was the local by-election, followed by 'Management and workers. And Britain. That's what I think'. A strain of latent imperialism was also emerging in his political identity; the question of 'What happens outside Britain?' provided:

Ben: Well, we've got soldiers stationed here, there and everywhere!

The laughter this provoked from the rest of the group was a response of some interest. Its basis was not clear but seemed to indicate that the idea was less than credible for the children. The permanence and stability of government, alongside the temporary nature of particular governments, was not a difficult idea for any of the children, in any age group, to understand and use. Here Ben used the idea of legitimate alternatives, and their necessity, to justify the party system as we know it. He accepted impermanent tenure of office as axiomatic, exemplified it by the Prime Minister's position, then extended the idea:

Ben: You know ... it's ... the Prime Minister. If he goes down then we change him. If a party starts failing, and not doing well at their job, then we change the party.

The limitations of the children's factual knowledge were apparent in the group's handling of the questions on the composition of Parliament.

Chris: Well, we all know about the House of Commons.

Q: You do?

Chris: Yes, all about that, the House of Commons, Houses of Parliament and House of Lords.

Q: Well, do you know what they do, in the House of Commons, Houses of Parliament and House of Lords?

Chris: That's a good question!

Q: Anybody know?

(Silence).

While children cannot be expected to analyse what it means to know 'all about' something, their own knowledge claims demonstrably need to be tested. Within his own limits of meaning, Chris was speaking truthfully, because to him 'knowing all about' the subject of Parliament was a very limited concept, and in having heard of it, knowing the geographical location and being able to recognise photographs, the possibilities were exhausted. The question of constructing relationships between Parliament and the recent local by-election did not arise for him. The availability of relevant information may well have not coincided with any feelings of interest or curiosity arising. His interest was aroused through the one piece of historic factual information he did possess:

Q: How do we get laws in this country?

Chris: Well, through the Kings, through the, er, ages we got laws.

Q: That was in history, wasn't it?

Chris: Yes, Henry VII, he made the jury of the twelve, didn't he?

Q: But how could we get a law this week, or next week?

Chris: Discuss it in one of the – Houses, would we? It would be the – House of Lords?

His willingness to go on was based on the possession of information, which guided his intuitive approach to new questions. His logic was based on the notion of law-giving as a royal function, which both influenced his choice of 'House of Lords' over 'House of Commons' as the law-making Assembly and created expectations of laws being granted from the wisdom of the rulers. Ben took another view, in direct contrast, giving his idea of the making of a law as a possible response to demands from the ruled.

Q: What kind of laws do you think we need in this country? Any new laws that you would like to make if you could?

Toni: No bombing and killing.

Ben: They should make a law, you know, all doing in protest – like bring back hanging. I think they should because then they'll stop killing and bombing. And, you know, then take it off again. If it starts again, make it and keep it.

Q: Would you like to learn more about politics at school?

Chris: Well, yes. We've got more ... er ... important things than politics in school, haven't you? You've got your job. You've got your education. And now, you know, in third years now, like this year ... what we're doing now will ... we'll really know what secondary school we'll go to.

He was confused and unsure about the processes of selection, but aware of the significance of work and curriculum priorities.

Q: So that's more important than learning about politics?

Ben: Yes.

He had of course made a fundamental political choice, which he was at that stage unable to recognise. An attitude had been adopted as a response to circumstances, in this case selection for secondary education at eleven-plus presenting ten-year-old children with the need for organising their priorities.

Comparison between this discussion and those of the other ten-year-olds reveals some common elements. The ten-year-old children appeared quiet, even self-contained, in comparison with the out-going self-confidence of the nine-year-olds. The reason for this may lie in the fact that they seemed to feel nothing like the same need for using large amounts of personal experience and anecdotes to construct examples of concrete situations. Some ten-year-olds were able to put forward particular points of view and to defend them consistently and to return to particular themes or interests to illustrate points required for various types of questioning. Stronger contact with realities of politics showed in some discussions, with considerably less attempt at speculation than children in the previous stage had shown. In contrast, there were many attempts by the children at rational justification and spontaneous classifying during answers in order, it appeared, to strengthen their personal systems of classification.

THE ELEVEN-YEAR-OLDS: CHILDREN AND CITIZENS

The eleven-year-old groups were strong on debate, often responding to a question by offering more information than had been asked for and elaborating freely on whatever interested them. With them, opinion is better-informed, appraisive. In these conversations they are able to develop a topic easily, keen to put forward points of view and to justify their claims and assertions. In short, the eleven-year-olds proved to have as much in the way of political ideas and intelligence and concern with issues as anybody else. They are changing into young adults, speaking for themselves, and in some of the extracts that follow we can see them moving on, politically, under the stimulus of discussion and argument.

We are listening to Charles, Babs, Mary and Keith, in South London, as Charles attempts a definition of the Labour Party:

Charles: It's a party of ... the working class. They believe that everybody should be equal.

Q: Can you tell me any more about it?

Charles: They believe in – equality. They think people should be given the same opportunities – they think people should all be the same, within reason. They believe – they just fight for the working class that are underpaid.

The attempt here was to unite principles of social action into a belief system and the use of 'believe' in preference to 'think', unsuccessful though it was, indicates that the boy had some awareness of the nature of ideological thinking. In the end he made do with the description, 'they just fight', which was a fall-back position from what he had set out to do.

Q: You know a lot about that. Where did you find out?

Charles: I'm quite interested in politics.

Q: How did you get interested?

Charles: Well, it started from the class election. From then I've really been interested. I've been following the Conservatives around Woolwich West.

Q: Do you like Mrs Thatcher?

Charles: I don't think she's got the drive. Men, they've got more drive in them. She's a bit too soft with people. She's got to be like Heath. Got to be tough against inflation. If people had been strong enough to fight against the miners, we would have been ... the inflation rate would have gone down considerably, but the Labour Party just give in 'cause they would lose their votes if they didn't give the right point increase.

Q: Do you know what inflation is? Do you know what it means?

Charles: De-valuation of the pound.

Q: What effects does it have? Do you know?

Charles: It's the cost of using money ... prices going up. And more wages being needed, for some people, so the pound gets less than it's worth – about 72 pence now.

Q: Can I ask you one more thing? You used the word 'equality'. What's 'equality'?

Charles: It is ... the same. People being the same and everybody – nobody's above anybody else.

Q: Do you think that's possible?

Charles: No. Because it would be dull ... life would be dull if there were no difference in ... qualities.

Q: But do you think equality could ever mean people not being the same. Or do you think it could be fair for people not to be the same?

Charles: I suppose ... I think it would be fair ... but I think everybody would prefer slight differences in qualities ... trouble is, you see, life is ever so dull. It would be as well – just like life in Russia is ... the same kind of clothes that they wear ... and it's all based upon equality.

Q: What do you think equality means, Keith?

Keith: Equal rights for everybody.

Q: What is it, to have a right?

Keith: Everybody's got ... if somebody's got something, somebody else has. It's fair to have someone else having the same ... and ... you know, working for it.

Q: You mean like equal shares?

Keith: Yes.

Q: I see. Now can you let these girls come back, about women (the two girls had obviously wanted to come in earlier on the question of 'drive' linked with sex, but they had contented themselves with grimaces at that point) and politics, and Mrs Thatcher?

Mary: I think that the way men always get twice as much money than the ladies get ... and I think the ladies should be paid less ... I mean more ... and I think Mrs Thatcher would be a good Prime Minister.

Babs: (Interrupting) Well, she knows about housework, she knows about prices of food ... men don't ... What about Shirley Williams and all those other people. They all know about food.

Charles: They don't ...

Babs: How do you know that they don't?

Charles: They don't – they have people to find out for them. About the wages for the same job, it's been changed now.

Babs: (Interrupting) It takes its time, doesn't it?

Charles: (Continuing his theme) A man gets the same as a woman would, working as say a cook or something like that. They get the same amount of money.

Mary: If you were in a factory, and the lady was doing the same job as a man, you wouldn't, you wouldn't find the man was getting the least.

Babs: Supposing the man's working for how much – the woman's working for how many, say they're in a glass factory, how many glasses she produces ... yes! She gets money for it – and, the man just gets paid. If she does about a hundred a day she'll probably get more money than the man.

Charles: Well, Margaret Thatcher, about the prices of food. What about all the taxes ... the men have got? And ... (pause to think).

Babs: Well, I personally, I think women and men should have equal rights because when the ladies get home they've got to do everything, while the men just sit down, or go to the pub, or something. And they've got to look after the children, and half of them just don't get the chance to go to work. And if they do, they get less than everyone else. And men get more, usually.

Mary: It's like my Mum. She can't get a job. You know, she's so bored at home. And she tried everywhere to get a job ... my Dad thinks she should go to his. But she won't agree, 'cause she won't get half as much money as he will.

Keith: Well, my Mum, she only works part-time, and she gets as much pay, as what a full-time secretary has. Because, in the time she has, from half-past nine to half-past three, she ... she does about as much work as what some ordinary secretaries would do, and she gets just as much as what they do.

Babs: Yes, how much does your Mum get, though? My Dad gets ...

Q: (Interrupting) No, no secrets!

(The children laughed. They were quite uninhibited about finances, and prepared to use family examples to illustrate their points. Mary was obviously about to build her argument on the relative pay of men and women, while Kevin appeared to have missed her point.)

Q: Listen, coming back to this fairness thing. You might say this – that a man has really got to pay, you know, for the food, and for the mortgage and support everybody – so men would say that they've got to work, and so it's fair they should have more. And they can say that women can stay at home if they want to. What about that?

Babs: It's not fair to the women, then. They just get bored at home doing everything at the same time every day.

Mary: Supposing they like it, though? Supposing they enjoy it?

Babs: My Mum don't!

Charles: A lot of women do like it.

Babs: Mine don't!

Charles: When my Mum, didn't used to go to work any more, she said it was a bliss working at home with your feet up on the table ... (Indignant interruption from both girls, the words of which were lost but the reaction unmistakable.)

Q: Let's come back to politics then. Babs's going to tell us about the state of the country.

Babs: Yes, the country's in such a state that women have to try to go to work or get a job to pay for all the – all the prices, that are going up, and all inflation.

Q: What do you think that people who rule the country, you know, like the Prime Minister, should do about these problems? Has anybody got any ideas about that one?

Babs: They should keep rules.

Keith: They should cut down on, er ... taxes, and things like that. We'd have more money to spend on other things except for bills and things like that.

Q: Yes. Now whose job is it to do these things? Anybody know?

Charles: I think it's the Prime Minister's. I think that taxes should be brought down and rates taken down, and cut down building roads, because the government, they don't really know what they're doing with our money. 'Cause it's our money; they – they say it's theirs, but it's our money they're spending. There's ... building racing stands with the money ... that's done by the Council sometimes. You know, we ought to be doing something useful to the country, not entertainment. I think we should get the country back on it's feet, and then get the entertainment right.

Q: You all think that, do you?

(Chorus of proffered examples of 'over-spending' which were not clearly linked with public sector.)

Babs: My Dad's got two cars, and one of them just sits there – my Mum's learning to drive, but ...

Q: But the government didn't give them to him, did they?

Babs: I know, but they should cut – they should ration their cars.

Charles: Do you mean they should stop your Dad from having two cars?

Babs: Yes.

Charles: Yes.

Babs: They should ration cars, now, so that there's only a certain amount sold a year, so that, I mean, say one person gets one in – five years. Like my Dad, last year, before that he got two in two years. He's got another one now.

Mary: I agree as well. Because if you cut down on cars, then people will have more money to spend on other things. It's a bit stupid having two cars in one family.

Charles: I think that cars – you know, the industry of cars, should be cut down, because there's loads of cars just standing in their workshops.

Q: And you think it's the Prime Minister's job to do this kind of thing? Well, could he do it all by himself?

Charles: I think, I think, perhaps no ... he has aides, and all the government; I think, you know, the Minister for Industry ... he should be ... they should cut down on the industry itself. I know there'd be a higher unemployment. That's inevitable. Unemployment's going up all the time.

Q: Do you know anything about the way government works?

Keith: Well, the Prime Minister has got people to ... in charge of, things and they get ideas about how to make this country a better place, and tell it to the Prime Minister and he does as much as possible, to make it possible, to make the country a better place; but half the time he gets all the ideas, and they're just pushed to one side, and things like the Common Market come first and .. we've got to think about our own country before we think about doing anything for Europe and things like that.

Q: When you say he does as much as possible – do you know what that 'doing as much as possible' consists of? What would the Prime Minister do if people gave him good ideas, do you know?

Charles: Ideas – about mining and industry.

Q: Yes, but what would he do?

Charles: Well, I think he's got all these aides to help him do what ... he could get all the other people – they're quite easily contacted, and he could get them to do these industries, that could be done, you know.

Q: Would he have to make some new laws, before he could do some of these things? How would he go about making a new law?

Charles: Well, he could get the Cabinet. And then ... if the cabinet agrees, then I suppose, it comes to the lower end.

Q: Well, do you know what happens when a law goes into the Houses of Parliament; it starts from the House of Commons. Do you know what happens then?

Keith: It has to be confirmed first.

Q: When?

Keith: In ... House of Lords.

Q: Then what happens?

Keith: It ... I'm not sure what they do next, but ...

Q: Have you ever heard of 'giving readings' to a bill, before it becomes law?

Keith: Yes. In Parliament.

Q: Yes. What about the Queen? What does the Queen do in all this? Anybody know?

Charles: She's only there as a tourist attraction. But I think she should ... there should ... be a Queen. Or a King.

Q: Why?

Charles: 'Cause ... it builds up the tourist trade ... 'cause all these Yankees ... they just come to see the Queen. That's their main thing in London. They come and see the Queen in all her glory.

Q: You don't think she does any work?

Babs: Yes!

Charles: She does quite a good job, diplomatically, with social relations, and things like that. I think she does a good job there. She doesn't really do much help though – politic-wise. Apart from signing papers and things like that.

Q: Is it important she should sign papers?

Babs: Yes.

Charles: Yes, I think so.

Q: Why do you think she has to sign papers?

Charles: Because she's Head of State. It's signed by England, put it that way, it's signed by common ...

Keith: I think ... she's kind of ... foreign secretary. She goes to other countries. You know to make – she's – in a way, she travels with England and she'd go to other countries to make friends with them, so, you know – they'd communicate with each other, and they'd be more help ... we'd be more help to them, they'd be more help to us ... I think that's the way she does it.

Q: You think that's a good job?

Charles: Yes.

Q: What about you, Mary?

Mary: Well, I think that Keith's right in saying that, that she does a good job by travelling around the countries, and getting up our trade, but – well – take, in Queen Victoria's time, she ruled the country, she governed it – the governors just took her ideas. No – you know – the Queen isn't any part. She just sends – sem – seminaries?

Q: What about you, Babs?

Babs: I think the Queen's very important because if she didn't sign the things then nobody could – the government couldn't really do it, because the government changes every now and again, and there'd be all different signatures and, the way she travels to other countries, you can't, you know, they could make war or something. When she travels to them if they're friendly, they're not likely to make war with us or anything.

Q: Yes, I see. That's very important, isn't it? Do you know what we call this country's form of government? We say 'It's a something-or-other'. Do you remember the word?

(No response.)

Q: We say 'Britain is a ...'?

Mary: Economical?

Q: No – a democracy. Have you ever heard that word, democracy?

(Children look doubtful.)

Q: Has anybody got any idea what it means?

Keith: What's the word?

Q: Democracy.

Keith: Mm ... democratic?

Q: Yes? We describe things as being democratic?

Charles: Well, they're ... well done.

Q: Well done?

Charles: Like the Queen. That's what I'm thinking of. We are very traditional, with our ways. We have these – traditions.

Q: Is Russia democratic?

Keith: I think so. With their – Heads of State, and their – big country.

Q: If I said to you that 'democratic' is a word that means rule by the people?

Keith: I think it is.

Charles: I think England is democratic, because the Common Market is done by peoples ... and the people decide who are candidates who they want to represent them.

Keith: My Dad said that if – when England do go in, the Common Market as they are, if they pulled up their socks and stood on their feet, and they could be the head country of ... 'cause then, they're not – some people regard us as a silly little island up in the Atlantic – or somewhere – and they think – just because we're that little island we're not that powerful ... But, why are we called Great Britain? That's what I think!

Q: What about you girls? Do you think this country's democratic?

Mary: It is – the Queen didn't decide the government. We all put a vote towards it, who we want, if we want, if there's a by-election, or something, we decide, the people coming to rule, by putting their vote in whoever they want to be in charge.

Babs: I think the same as well. In a lot of countries, people are just put in, by Kings or Queens, and the people in the country, they just don't like people when they go against them, and that country just goes barmy.

Q: I see. Have you got any political leanings? You know, are you Labour or Conservative or Liberal, or anything?

Charles, Babs and Mary: Conservative!

Keith: Labour!

Q: Have you got any idea why?

Babs: Labour, some of them are Communist. Liberal just don't get in ever, and they're not strong enough.

Q: What about Mary – why are you a Conservative?

Mary: Well, Liberal – I never think of Liberal aren't nearly strong enough, they haven't got nearly enough seats. And they couldn't rule the country. And Labour, they've got Communists and everything in them, I don't like Labour.

Keith: I think – Conservative and Labour are doing a good thing, they're fighting for rights for other people. And Labour confirming them – you know. They take Conservatives' ideas and put them into other ways, for the people.

Charles: I believe in Conservatives, mainly because I don't like the Labour Party. They're going to, sometime, in the near future, they're going to go Communist. They got too strong a left wing.

The children here were making attempts to deal with the relationships between political ideas; as each made an attempt to construct an argument involving their analysis, it became necessary to relate the initial propositions to more complex ideas. They showed varying abilities to sustain a line of thinking, the most successful effort coming from Charles.

The concept of a political party, only loosely united ideologically, containing 'too strong a left wing' with a Prime Minister 'leaning towards the Conservatives' is a sophisticated one for an eleven-year-old, as is the style of argument employed. Charles showed an ability to construct a rational hypothesis in his last sentences, producing evidence to support his statement and explaining its relevance. The fact that his explanation was incomplete is less surprising than his ability to think in these terms, particularly in spontaneous discussion.

Q: What do you think is the difference between the Labour Party and the Communist Party?

Charles: There's hardly any difference ... perhaps the Labour Party aren't as strict as Communists, and the Communists fight more – a lot more, for their party and ... the Labour Party, they have got some right wing, which you know, believe in Conservative ways a bit, like Harold Wilson. I think he's going just like a Conservative at the moment, apart from all this nationalisation and things. I think he's going – he's leaning – towards the Conservatives. It showed in the Common Market referendum. He was – his campaign was a lot – with the Tories.

Q: What is it about politics that interests you?

Charles: Well, it's mainly the elections ... I find quite interesting – you know. I'm usually, when there's an election going on, I'm usually up about 5 o'clock in the morning.

Q: Are you? Can you all do that?

Keith, Babs and Mary: No.

Babs: I think before it ... they really ... you know ... they go mad, trying to get people to vote for them.

Mary: It's interesting hearing them talk, and fight for their – rights and things like that ... and the way these women go into Parliament and, you know, start to kick up a row ... about rights.

Babs: I think, things like political viewcasts (broadcasts) where they have a certain party, they just do no good, because each week they have a different person. And – everybody knows who they are – everybody knows what they do and yet sit there on telly and show what they can do. All they do is sit behind a desk just nattering on. And it's barmy.

Q: Do you believe what they say?

Babs: No!

Mary: In the by-elections, the only time you see people is when there's going to be an election, like — came down our road and came to our house about two days before the election. He'd never come before. And then there was Labour and Liberal leaders coming down to people's houses. You know, just to get them to vote for them.

Q: What do you think the Government ought to do, at present. You know, are there any particular things that you think Government ought to do?

Charles: Yes, I think inflation should be brought down by – I think – there should be a wage freeze that should be in for about two years and then, the government should just restrict wages after that.

Q: Do you think everybody should stay as they are?

Charles: I think the country should just suffer the prices for a while. I think it'd be worth it for their children – for their future.

Q: Do you think the government we have now, and the way we run the country now is the best way we could, or do you think there are, you know other ideas?

(General attempts to answer this question all at once.)

Q: Can we have one at a time? Who wants to start?

Charles: Me. I think that there should be a government that fights for themselves and fights for the country. I think the Labour party are fighting for themselves with the miners, because they can't say they want more money. And they shouldn't do, because they only give it for their own votes, the Labour party. For their own votes, which is to fight inflation, so they say – the prices are just going up and up. And the wages are going up and up.

Q: Do you think the way we run the country is the best way we could run it, or are there any other ideas that you'd like to see in the government – you know, different? Perhaps not a Prime Minister, perhaps two or three people?

Charles: No. I think there should be one Prime Minister, but I don't think he should make all the decisions. I think his ministers should make certain decisions unless the Prime Minister really does disagree with them.

Q: Does he make all the decisions, do you think?

Charles: Well, the ministers have to have his con ... have his – permission, virtually always.

Q: Do you think the Queen should play a bigger part?

Charles: Yes.

Keith: Yes.

Charles: I think she's capable of doing a good job.

Keith: I think these people who are – high, in power – like all the judges, and the Prime Minister, and the MPs and the Queen. They should act together, and they shouldn't really have Labour Party and Conservative Party and Liberal Party. I think they should all work together. I think that would make the world a better place.

Q: Do you know what that's called, when people drop their party labels and work together?

Charles: Coalition!

Q: That's right.

Charles: They had that during the war.

Q: Yes?

Charles: But it was pretty well dominated by the Conservatives – because it was Churchill who was Conservative, and it was pretty well dominated by them.

Q: He was a strong leader, wasn't he? Do you think it's important to have a strong leader?

Charles: Yes, very good.

Keith: Yes.

Babs: Yes.

Mary: Sir Winston Churchill was our Prime Minister (changes subject). I don't think they should bring in these new foods like Womble jellies. I mean, they're just wasting sugar.

Babs: Yes, I mean there's ordinary jellies. Just because Womble jellies are in a different packet, it doesn't mean anything, they're just wasting more – more sugar, more everything.

Mary: And new washing powders. We could do without them before, and look at the new sweets, and everything. It's just making everything – you know, you're buying more, when you see new stuff come out.

Q: Does somebody want to say something about leaders?

Keith: I think – Mr Heath – you know, goes round – individual – I think he should do more things for politics because he isn't a stupid leader. He was a good leader, and if Mr Heath, Mrs Thatcher and ... Mr Wilson work together, I think, we'd have a stronger country.

Q: You all mentioned Winston Churchill. Do you know much about Winston Churchill?

Babs: He was a good leader. He put the country on their feet and he had special ways of getting to people and telling them what's happening when the war was on.

Mary: About ten years before the war between Germany and England, he went over to Germany and told the people that they were going to fight against us. Nobody would believe him so they chucked him out. Then ten years later the war did come and they all depended on him. And he doesn't – he didn't – he never wanted us to be in the Common Market.

Q: How do you know all this?

Mary: Before the Common Market, by-election – was on – it was on (TV) about the Common Market. He didn't want us to be in the Common Market.

Charles: Churchill, if he was alive now, he would have voted to stay in the Common Market, because it would have been for the good of the country, and I think he would have said 'Yes'. Because he boosts people's morale. During the war he was always encouraging people. He said – you know – for the good of their country and their children, just fight on and never surrender.

Q: Yes, I see. And you like Winston Churchill as well, Keith?

Keith: Yes. He was a good fighter. I think that's how we got our name Great Britain. And that's how it – this country, ever since the war, has been a powerful country. But since he's died, they've just slacked, and they've just fallen to pieces. We haven't had any really powerful men like – or a woman – like him. We need better – someone like him. There have been other women in his time. They've been trying to be powerful.

Q: Women?

Keith: Yes. That's Emily Pankhurst and all these women who just flung themselves in front of cars and horses, and things like that. They think that's the way to get power, but I don't think that's right. I think they should do it in a different way.

Q: Yes, I see. When you say 'get power' – who does it belong to? What is power? Who knows what power is?

Charles: Dominating the country. That's what I think the Labour Party are doing. They're just dominating the country. I know they gave us the vote for the EEC, but, they're just too strong. And ...

Q: We'll come back if you've forgotten that bit. Would you like another election soon?

Charles: Yes.

Mary: Well, I think that we – we've got some old people who are really getting on in the government. I think we should have new people in, young people, who know about the country, and know what state it's in. They know what to do. But old people can't – they just can't do anything!

Q: But Winston Churchill was old, and you liked him!

Babs: Ah, but he started being Prime Minister when he was young – about 26!

Q: Do you think so?

Mary: Well, he started as a general or something.

Keith: An MP, and he worked his way up there.

Mary: But you know people like Harold Wilson, they've just suddenly come in.

Q: I think he's been around quite a time. Tell me this, would you like to be MPs when you grow up?

Charles, Keith and Mary: No.

Q: You wouldn't, Charles? Although you're interested in politics?

Charles: No. I'd like to have a fairly highly paid job, but I just couldn't stand up to the criticism you'd get. That's the only thing I admire all these MPs for, is the criticism they take.

Keith: I wouldn't like to be one. Because of the newspapers. They put –

you say something, like last night, I saw these ... journalists, writing down. There was one man, he was just writing down all the important parts. He was probably writing down things that Mr Callaghan had never said. That's what I think's wrong with newspapers.

Charles: I think there's too much intrusion into MPs' lives – private lives.

Q: Do you think so?

Charles: I think religion's got a lot to do with it – in most of our – political parts. I think religion – the Church of England and the Queen – has got a lot to do with the politics. I don't think the country's too religious. I think it should be a bit more religious than what it is.

Q: What about the girls? Would you like to be an MP when you grow up?

Mary: No.

Q: Why?

Babs: Because Margaret Thatcher was saying on telly that she'd had everyone putting different things in the newspaper ... and I just wouldn't like it – everybody getting mad at you and they'd hate you.

Mary: I'd hate to be an MP because you've got no private life at all. Wherever you go, there's newspaper reporters there – then every day there'd be something about you in the newspaper, and some of the stuff they write about you isn't true!

Q: Supposing you could say one thing for the country, to do for it, that the government ought to do. What would you choose?

Keith: I think they should – cut the country up, and they should look over that country – over that part of the country. Like cut them into states and then excavate (investigate?) into it – find out about it, and then see what's happened in the last past – decade – in the last ten years, and I think that's the only way we can find out more about our country.

Charles: I agree with Keith. I think we should get a certain part of the country or a certain industry, and get that perfect, or as perfect as we can get it and then go on to another industry. I know it would be a slow process, but it would be probably the only way it could be done. 'Cause if you do it all in one go, it'd be a hopeless task.

Keith: They should excavate it all at once – all at once!

Mary: I think they should cut all the country into about five parts or so many parts, and then get certain leaders that are strong and a few people behind him, and they should put a person, and a few other people, in charge of each part of the country and then they should run it like we run England. Then our policemen wouldn't have such a job trying to get all over, quickly, and the Prime Minister would still be in charge of our country as well.

Babs: I think we should start with East London first, because that's a terrible part of England. Everywhere you go there's litter all over and there's not many people – housed or anything. Then they should go to London and other parts like that, you know, where there's not too many people housed. And I think instead of making roads, and everything, they should have more greenery around, because it makes it look nicer.

Keith: You know how beautiful the Lake District is? Well, that's got copper, tin, iron ore. It's got some gold and silver. It's got all the things we need. But, you know, the government are so greedy, they just want to wipe out all England's beauty and things like that. And take away all these forests, with iron and things being brought out of it. I think we've got enough iron as it is, from other parts, like Wales, and the slate-mines there where they find iron and things like that. But we don't need to burst into the Lake District where most of it is. It's uninhabited, most of it. I think if you did that, you wouldn't get tourists in England, and England wouldn't have as much money as what they would ... because they'd need money to – investigate – it and, you know, take the iron and the copper ...

Babs' contribution on a specific area – East London – linked with questions of housing and control of road construction, was taken on into aspects of environment and conservation, accurately illustrated geographically and geologically by Keith. Economic justifications were produced; the children were able to move beyond mere description and to see that arguments required relevant justification.

The arguments, while not profound (for example, ignoring of industrial relationships) still showed internal coherence, and the contribution of each child provided a logical further stage in the general coherence of the discussion. Keith's use of the word 'excavate' for 'investigate' was unimportant in the context, for the word was accepted on his terms and endowed with his meaning and purpose – an example of the 'exchange value' of language in action.

This last section, it is suggested, is of great significance for the case presented in this work, for it provides an active moment in children's development in political understanding. Motivated by their agreement about alternative possible futures, they were able to focus together on one idea. In organising their information into a particular framework and presenting the ideas as aspects of a total theme they achieved a community of political imagination. Different cognitive styles did not prevent this; Charles' dawning ability to think within the logic of a discipline underpinned Keith's original creative leap. Mary's focus on organisation and Fabian retention of the traditional power-base ('and the Prime Minister would still be in charge of our country as well'), and Babs' subjective approach (a sign that she was not yet as ready as the others, in their different ways, to deal with abstractions), added further dimensions. Politics, throughout this wide-ranging discussion was not departed from, but given a wide interpretation.

It is suggested that this section of the discussion marks the optimum point in the children's development of political concepts. It came at the end of a session which may well have provided opportunities for development during its course by setting up 'problem-solving' situations to which the children responded with great interest. Without this element of motivation it is possible for a discussion with children of this age to take a very different form and atmosphere, in which responses are minimal, as was the case with the two eleven-year-old girls recorded earlier in Essex. In that instance politics was not accepted as a worthwhile discussion topic and little motivation was generated.

The last group of eleven-year-olds that I want to present in conversation we have already met – as nine-year-olds. So, after this lapse of time we join Janet, Jamie and Marcus again as they begin to talk about what aspects of politics they find interesting. They had started from a politics-as-fun, jokey level, swopping stories and different versions of: 'Did you see so-and-so impersonating — on this TV programme?' when suddenly Marcus changed the mood. Having told a joke against an ex-President of the United States, he then added, when the laughter subsided, 'Poor chap. He's wasting his time.' And the giggles ended. We went on from there to the details of what interested them:

Jamie: ... things to do with school, dinner money going up, and sometimes they change the holidays, and things like that, and all the elections.

Marcus: I like the bits I can understand.

Q: What are they?

Marcus: Well, there's the elections. I understand how they happen and why. There's the reshuffle of the Cabinet. If somebody died, he'd reshuffle them. And I like to get to know the people on television – see what they're like, hear them talk, see what their attitude is to the world. You know, like some people have different views and see how they mix it together. And I try to form an idea with two people, one saying one view, and the other the other, and I like to try and mix them so that they become equal, and yet still do good for the country.

Q: And do you make up your mind what you think about it?

Marcus: Yes.

Q: Janet?

Janet: Well, I like watching the programmes 'Today' and 'Nation-wide', I think they're very interesting. The education things – when they talk about when they used to hit the children. I used to listen to things like that because they used to say: 'You shouldn't hit children, you should hit children'. It was quite complicated, but it was very good. I enjoyed it a lot. I don't watch a lot. I don't like watching the news very much, but I like watching 'Nationwide' and 'Today', it's all I really like watching.

Q: Are you interested in problems, the problems the country has?

Janet: I got a bit annoyed about that.

Q: What did you get annoyed about?

Janet: All the people unemployed and all the jobs they have ...

Janet was not quite sure what she wanted to do here, beyond registering some kind of protest, and it seemed she was not quite ready, at this point, to make the move from using 'cosy' examples and illustrations, to dealing impersonally with issues. Jamie tried to pick up her line of thinking and attempt an explanation:

Janie: It's about the pound's ... going down ... because it's gold, isn't it? The gold's going down, so is the money, the gold which you need for the money.

Here Jamie seemed to have grasped the principle involved, and a set of economic relationships. Janet had not, and she moved the discussion straight back to her preferred territory:

Janet: On grammar schools. My brother went to a grammar school, and my Mum wanted me to go to a grammar school. But they're all tied in with the ILEA (Inner London Education Authority) and the ILEA don't want grammar schools now. So we don't really know what to do. My Mum has to send me to a comprehensive school now, but she really wants the grammar standard. See, my brother goes to an independent one now, a totally independent type of grammar, and it was really hard. They give nice good dinners there, he says things like 'chicken and chips' and all things like that.

Q: Do you want to go to the school that gives the best dinners?

Janet: Yes! And the best education. In other schools, the comprehensive and secondary modern, they've got some more practical things like metalwork and woodwork and housecraft. And if you want to you can do knitting or something.

Q: Who should choose, do you think?

Janet: Whoever knows best about it.

Q: Who do you think that might be?

Janet: Well, your parents really, I should think.

Strong support came in here from Marcus, who was able to develop Janet's 'knowing best' into specific areas and justifications:

Marcus: I think they should be able to tell what's best because they've, if you'll pardon the expression, they've lived on the earth longer than I have, and know the area in which we live more than, better than, I do. They know all the advanced stuff about school.

Q: Do you think education has got anything to do with politics?

Janet: Well I suppose, because we've got to know, if we're having discussions like this. If we were older, in secondary schools, or if we went to college, we should be able to discuss about education as they should. They go mad on politics on 'Today', you know, they shout sometimes, about politics and education, and all things that should happen. And we should all have a say over them really.

Q: We should all have a say?

Janet: Yes. They all have, in secondary schools. They have government and politics.

Q: What problems do you think we have in this country?

Marcus: Well, there's trying to pay the IMF loan back.

Q: Do you understand something about that?

Marcus: Well, the unemployment, all the strikes British Leyland and the steel manufacturers are having, it's brought Britain into ruin, so they had to get a loan from a company, a firm called the IMF, International Monetary Fund, to lend us some money. So we've got the money, and we're having difficulty trying to pay it back now.

Q: Do you know much about other countries, in politics?

Janet: I think I know much more because I went on the school journey to Wales. I know the clothes and all things like that, but I don't know the politics of people in Wales.

Marcus: The Devolution Bill. If the Bill gets through the House of Commons.

Q: Have you got any ideas about that?

Marcus: I think it would be a good way for Scotland and Wales if they could have their own government, but not too much power, otherwise England would be over-ruled. There'd be arguments with England, say against Scotland, and then Wales might take sides and then have a stronger body, Scotland and Wales, put together would be about the size of England. The bodies of ministers, and the Welsh and Scottish governments would be strong enough, if they picked the best politicians of their country, to battle and defeat a Bill in the House of Commons, because they would have a say, if the Bill was to do with the whole United Kingdom.

Q: Because that's democratic?

Marcus: Yes.

Q: When I use that word 'democratic', do you know what I mean?

Jamie: Yes. It means everybody, they have their choice. Not like the Communists. The Communists, they've just got the politicians to vote for them, but in this country, being democratic, the people get their vote. It's fairer really. It's what the people want.

Q: Marcus?

Marcus: I just think that it's fair that we should be able to vote freely and have our own pick, because if we think somebody's good, we vote for them and give them a chance.

Q: Janet, the boys used words like 'free' and 'fair' when they were talking about democracy. Do you think that's what democracy is?

Janet: Well, I'm not sure, because the Queen, she's Queen of our country, isn't she? But the Government seem to rule the country more than what even the Queen does. I think the Queen should have even more say. In anything, all the problems in the world.

Jamie: The Queen is just a monarch though, now, since Oliver Cromwell. It changed.

Janet: She's just left on the side.

Q: Why do we have a Queen?

Janet: Tradition? It's about the only thing, I suppose.

Marcus: Well, she does sign all the Bills after they've gone through the House. That's about all she does do with politics.

Janet: I think it's better, really, to have a Queen. Not one who's hard and things like that, and horrid to you. But when they can be fair about things and judge it rightly.

Q: Whichever party is in power?

Janet: Yes.

Q: When I say that, 'whichever party is in power', what do I mean?

Marcus: Well, in this case, the Labour government's in power. When I was watching the news last night, there didn't seem much to me that the

Labour back-benchers could do in the government. It was all the Cabinet Ministers who were running the things. I don't see the reason why we should have the gigantic bodies of people doing nothing except voting to try to get the government to do what they want to do.

Jamie: It won't be any good now because the government will be outvoted soon.

Q: You think it will?

Jamie: Yes. You've got the Conservatives and Liberals and all the others ganging up.

Q: In what ways do you think the Conservatives might have different ideas from the Labour party?

Jamie: First of all, about schools. The Conservatives, they won't be able to change it when they come in. It will take a long time, and we'll have left school by then. The Conservatives want grammar schools, but the Labour want comprehensives.

Marcus: I've always liked the Conservative party. I think Mr Healey's done well in his job as best he could. He's trying to bring the country back.

Q: What is Mr Healey?

Marcus: The Chancellor of the Exchequer. I think the load, the burden, after the re-shuffle last night, the burden will be taken off his back because there's an executive from the Treasury who's been taken into the Cabinet to help him, so he'll have a greater say than he would have done.

Q: I read somewhere that he would have liked to be Prime Minister. Do you think so?

Marcus: Yes. It said on television he would like to become Foreign Secretary. I think he's been every other minister except. But it would be so difficult six weeks before the budget.

Q: Do you know who is Foreign Secretary, Jamie?

Jamie: He deals with all the foreign current affairs, all the signing of documents making peace, like with Iceland, the Cod War. If they make peace he'd probably go out there and make sure that it's safe.

Q: Do you know the name of the man who has that job now?

Marcus: Dr David Owen, MP.

Q: What kind of things do you think he should do?

Marcus: Well, I think they ought to have a go and try to settle the Rhodesian problem and the South African one, because South Africa and Rhodesia were British provinces and I think we should have a great deal of say in trying to do it, but they won't listen to us.

Q: Jamie, what do you think the Government should be doing?

Jamie: It's in quite a state at the moment. They've lost nearly all the Empire, so we're not an Empire any more. I wish they could hang on to a few things.

Q: Would you like to be politicians, when you grow up?

Marcas: I've got greater ambitions than an MP. I'd like to help rule the country. If it was still in ruin when I became a politician, I would like to be able to get into the Cabinet, make a name for myself, and try to help the country back on its feet, because I think it will still be in this state. I think I'd like to get the country back on its feet if I could now. I'm only eleven at the moment so I couldn't do much now.

Q: Jamie, would you like to be an MP when you grow up?

Jamie: No, I don't think I really would. But if I did, I'd like to make it more civil, make the world more civil in its rights.

———————————

I have attempted to re-create in the preceding pages what happened when a few groups of children, quite ordinary children you might meet in any Primary School classroom, who happened to be available at the time, were brought together and encouraged to talk about their ideas of politics. They spoke only for themselves, neither as representatives of any group or class, nor as 'typical' of anything – even childhood. For 'typical' children are as mythical as unicorns, and 'the child', that handy theoretical figure, is a prop that most of us who are interested in children can do without. Which is to say that I wish to attempt no inductive leaps in the form of general conclusions; the children under discussion are the ones I have encountered. I am not, as it were, moving from them by way of a 'therefore', to the total offspring of mankind. So the conclusions that it seems useful to offer at this point, before going on to consider a wider range of written responses from larger groups of children, are really questions. They are the inevitable questions that arise out of what the children were able to do, and they are complex.

First a premise. It seems possible to claim that many children take an interest in, and enjoy talking about, political events and personalities of the day, and that they come to have a grasp of issues and principles. And one might ask 'Why not? Isn't this a very easy thing to do – needing no skills except language, no experience except that of being in the world? Don't children "pick up" political ideas in much the same way as they "pick up" the language, by listening and imitating?'

The comparison with language is a useful one. Children are, obviously, born with the capacity for acquiring language skills. As we all know, the acquisition of language is an incredibly complex achievement. The fact that, at an early age, children have usually gained sufficient skill to construct their own meaningful sentences does not diminish the complexity of the task, but leads us to try to examine exactly what it is that they are able to do. We find, not a limited imitative ability dependent on models, but a creative faculty that takes language as a tool.

'Look, Mummy, – dead bread!' said my small daughter once as we were feeding the ducks. Mouldy crusts were littering the ground. But 'dead bread'? Probably every parent in the world can make lists of this kind of chat, fully realising that children are creating something of their own. Its significance is seen in Chomsky's (1967) proposition that we possess, as a species, an innate capacity for acquiring the structures of language, for in this view we are not merely imitators, dependent on models, but capable of exploring possibilities of our own.

This brings me to the important question of whether we possess, in the same idiom, an innate capacity for the 'grammar' of politics, of understanding some basic things about social organisation and the nature of group membership? The notion of such an innate capacity – or category – appears feasible for reasons that are, to some extent, demonstrated in the previous section. Firstly, the nature of the responses from the youngest children is of interest, for they include ideas, albeit unsophisticated in expression, that show them to be in possession of principles that give meaning and relevance to actions, and enable certain kinds of meaning and action to be designated 'political'. We might want to ask whether these categories or principles have been taught to the children, and here the answer must surely be that this would not be possible, at least in terms of any kind of direct teaching. Any attempt to do so would be regarded as educationally ludicrous – a facade for indoctrination.

Secondly, with a number of the children, there seemed to be an ability to understand the essentials of what was being communicated, often in spite of imperfect articulation. They were able to help each other make ideas explicit, often without further assistance.

Thirdly, the expansion of ideas was rapid, given the right stimulus, which may have been a question, a word, or the struggle to find one. Looked at another way, the discussion itself can be regarded as an extended stimulus, and in this respect it is interesting to see the style of responses, at the second interview, of the children who had been involved in a similar interview two years previously. As a group, these children seemed to be in closer contact with the day-to-day events and realities of the political scene, more at terms with the world as it is. This indication, which at present cannot be regarded as more than that, implies that the stimulus of discussion was a strong and lasting one. Its nature was to 'draw out', not to attempt to teach, and the fact that this was successful carries implications for the kind of mental tasks involved. The implications for any possible teaching are also strong, and I shall return to these at a later stage.

4

Reflections on paper

A much larger number of children can be involved in writing responses to questions than can be brought into discussion groups, and it would hardly have been possible to have talked with all 800 children who participated by working through questionnaires. Using both approaches seemed desirable, in order to achieve both depth and breadth in the study. (Further details of the questionnaire are to be found in the Appendix.) I have kept, quoting verbatim, some of the children's idiosyncratic expressions and spellings, particularly where they seem to show a child's effort or ingenuity in organising limited skills to communicate his thoughts. The range of topics is expanded. In addition to the aspects of politics that the children in the discussion groups talked about, ideas about freedom, authority, rules and rule-keeping are included. Traced throughout the age-range, this set of ideas provides our starting-point.

CHILDREN'S OPINIONS OF SCHOOL RULES

Children are trained to obey some rules; even in the most democratic institution the rules of safety are indispensable, and those of essential administration usually considered so. Rules also spell security; they enable children to satisfy authority, and to predict with some accuracy other people's behaviour. For some children rules give valuable clues for interaction, for understanding what is expected of them, and are a means for obtaining approval and reward. For others, they provide a challenge to energy and ingenuity. Children are used to being expected to support rules; they are not so used to being asked to explain why they do or do not support them. It is, therefore, of some interest to consider the children's own rationalisations of keeping school rules.

Is it important to keep the school rules? Why?

Mixed Junior School (London), seven-year-old girls:
Because it is safe and good.
Then you will not get told off.
Because they are important.
Because you might hurt your nose.
'cause you will get in a muddle.
Because you will get hurt.
I think it is because you will not get told off.

Mixed Junior School (London), seven-year-old boys:
Because otherwise everything would be in a muddle.
Because the school rules can help you.
To keep the school going.
Don't know.
Because you would get told off.
Because it will get ruf (sic).
Because they're important.

There is a firm link here between the idea of rules, and notions of order and security, and keeping out of trouble. Restraint appears to be accepted as a lesser evil than having others unrestrained; we are not told why 'you will get hurt'; whether the child fears being bullied, or perhaps inadvertently pushed in a scramble from one place to another, nevertheless, rules prevent behaviour by others which might result in personal hurt being suffered. The classroom then could be a jungle for some. For others it could be a mess, and rules are preferable to muddle. By age eight, more information is available:

Mixed Junior School (London), eight-year-old girls:
Because children will run about in the corridors and knock the smaller children over.

There is also another point of view – the emergence of institutional solidarity:
Because it would be disobeying the school and letting it down.

It will keep the School's good name.

An environmental hazard appeared in:

Sometimes you get watched.

Not keeping rules meant – you are not being sensible.

Because everyone else does.

Because all the school will then do the same.

Some saw no choice:

Because you've got to obey.

Mixed Junior School (London), eight-year-old boys:

Because you could cause an accident to other people.

Because there could be a fight.

The rules are to keep people from cheating.

You might disturb other classes.

It will keep you out of trouble.

For the boys in particular, it seems, rules are concerned with restraint of physical actions; freedom, conversely, will be the absence of physical restraint on this account. The girls are not so much concerned with their personal restraint, rather they see a world which has a natural propensity towards chaos.

The attraction of the idea of discarding rules is highest between the ages of nine and ten, according to the information collected. Some children would not discard rules on the grounds of 'you would not know what to do', 'you wouldn't learn anything', 'it wouldn't be the same'. The rebel elements simply preferred 'no work', 'I could read all the time' or 'because you would not have to take orders from anyone', and 'we would have more freedom'. From the reasons given for their choices, it would seem that between these ages of nine and ten, children become aware of the regulations of their own behaviour by the adult world's contingent rules. This consciousness becomes rationalised either in a decision to go along with the system: 'You get on better if you do', 'So I don't get told off', or with the conviction that without the security of a rule-governed existence, life would be unpleasant in some ways: chaotic and muddled or even dangerous. The resulting emotional commitment to rule-keeping is further rationalised, when questioned. Some children seem to need the aid of imagination in order to preserve or construct their commitment, after the age of about nine. After this age, simple cause and effect such as 'you will get told off' gives way to specific reasons, as demonstrated by ten-year-olds who supported rules because they 'stop accidents – screaming and shouting – getting in a mess', 'because you are embarrassed when told off', 'because you won't learn anything'.

Mixed Junior School (London), nine-year-old girls:

Because you don't get muddled up.

The school would not be very nice.

Because you know what you are doing.

Because no one fights with you.

Mixed Junior School (London), nine-year old boys:

Because if you did not the school would go to rack and ruin.

It would get in a terrible mess.

Get expelled.

To make a better school.

If you didn't there would be no disipln (sic).

Mixed Junior School (London), ten-year-old girls:

You would get in a mess.

There would be screaming and shouting.

So we all behave ourselves.

You will get told off.

(These are typical responses.)

Mixed Junior School (London), ten-year-old boys:

You will be safer.

It is not fair to the rest of the school.

Because people could go around with bombs.

The school would fall apart.

There would be chaos, no discipline.

If I don't I shall have a bad report and disappoint my parents.

Because the Headmistress says we have to.

Mixed Junior School (Kent), ten-year-old girls:

Because the school would look odd.

So you know what to do.

Accidents could happen.

So we do not have silly boys running about.

School would be untidy.

If you didn't keep the school rules you wouldn't know anything, so I keep to rules.

If everyone didn't keep the rules the school wouldn't be like a school.

Everyone in the school would be swearing and running down the corridors.

So everybody wears the same.

You get along better.

School will be much better.

Everybody be happy.

Mixed Junior School (Kent), ten-year-old boys:

Because if you fight there is no one to stop you.

Help us make a better school.

School would be in a riot.

So we do not go like a bad apple.

Different clothes look untidy.

If we didn't the school would be nothing but a dump and no one would do anything on time or anything any time.

Because some rules are stupid.

Mixed Junior School (London), eleven-year-old girls:

I think a school should have discipline.

My class would get in an uproar.

To help stop accidents.

It keeps things in order.

Mixed Junior School (London), eleven-year-old boys:

You might get hurt by knives.

You could get hurt.

Mixed Junior School (Kent), eleven-year-old girls:

If they didn't take any notice of the rules the school would be destroyed.

To keep a reputation.

You wouldn't know what to do.

You are likely to do all your work wrong.

Mixed Junior School (Kent), eleven-year-old boys:

We would have people getting knocked over.

It would be a place of riots.

Yes, the school will go mad without them.

So that you do not get violence.

The school would be a mass of junk.

There would be shouting in classrooms.

Fighting all the time.

The ten-year-olds in Kent provided a rather more imaginative set of reasons; it seemed that in a less authoritarian situation, the children produced stronger reasons for rule-keeping at this age. At age eleven, the unpleasantness of possible alternatives to rule-keeping had become more elaborated. Girls were rather more concerned now 'to keep a reputation'. For the boys, 'the school would go mad without them'. Rules exist for the sake of safety, but are also seen as instrumental, enabling work to be done and order to exist. There is not only passive acquiescence in this, but the elements of moral judgement; the objectives of schooling are endorsed.

Children, in their support for rules seem to fall into two basic categories; the strongly supportive, for whom the rules represent quality of life, and those who accept rules as part of a contingent situation, where conformity avoids unpleasantness in some form. These are basic attitudes which, internalised as a result of early educational training, will affect later political and social concept-building. It can be said that such attitude formation has particular elements of interest for political growth.

Firstly, children appear to have little urge to extend their own freedom of action in the school situation. They see freedom as a relative good, less attractive than security. Secondly, children accept given rules as moral values and construct value judgements accordingly. These value judgements concern collective versus individual rights and particular conceptions of the general good reputation, safety, security and even tidiness. Thirdly, crude forms of utilitarian ethics appear to operate for children. These are crude so long as the consequences of an action can only be guessed at or perceived intuitively. This utili-tarianism is based on peer-group membership, valued initially insofar as it does not conflict with a child's personal interests. Once he has transferred certain rights to the peer-group (for example, when a group as a whole make up rules for games to which all agree), he has entered into a basic democratic situation. The early, crude utilitarianism becomes the germ of perception of democratic processes. For children, this stage is signified by using any way of voting to make a group decision. This principle is internalised once a child, finding himself in the minority, can still accept the majority decision. Thus, through play and through school organisation, children learn two different concepts of rules: one active; one passive.

If the content of school rules at the Primary stage seems to have little connection with political concept building, a consideration of the principles involved can be revealing. What is at issue is usually the restraint of individual behaviour, that is, questions of individual and collective rights, the relationship of individual members to the group and the concomitant obligations.

In summary, from the answers of this group of children, it would appear that children, by the age of nine, are generally convinced that a rule-governed situation is essential to the preservation of order and safety; that in its absence life, if not actually short, might well be nasty and brutish. The great majority here are committed to the need for the rule of law, although the system has its occasional failures. 'Some rules are stupid' observed a non-conforming ten-year-old, exceptionally.

CHILDREN'S ASPIRATIONS TO LEADERSHIP AND RESPONSIBILITY IN THE SCHOOL

The positions of form captain and class monitors were found to exist in all the groups. The question, 'Would you like to be form captain?' was intended to investigate children's attitudes to the one position of authority which was available to them within the classroom. In many Junior schools a boy and/or a girl are elected by their classmates for these roles, which usually consist of being responsible, to some extent, for certain classroom tasks being performed, or standards of behaviour or quietness maintained, should the teacher be absent from the room.

The connection between this question and the next one 'Would you like to be *a* monitor?' is one of comparison, and concerns children's different attitudes towards being the form captain or class leader, and *a* responsible helper within the class group. Many children explained the latter preference by stating that they 'liked to help' generally, or liked particular jobs. The level of motivation towards this role rises with the ages of the children, in contrast with their desire for leadership and authority.

Power appears to be perceived by Primary children in two ways: there is the 'bossing' element, which some children cited as a reason for rejecting the form captain's role ('Because I do not want to boss people', 'They would call me "bossy-boots" '): and there is also the much more highly approved 'helping' or 'looking-after' that is projected on to government and public figures. It seems that more children are quite prepared to accept such a construction of power and authority, and to act as a member of a group with specific duties, than to act in a purely authoritative capacity – except when a school situation presents, implicitly or explicitly, the idea of power as desirable or as a reward.

Comparisons showed attitudes to authority and responsibility in school to differ between age- and sex-group. In particular, the age of nine years appeared to be of some significance. It represented the time of highest aspiration to authority for the girls in the mixed schools, and the lowest point for the girls in the single-sex school. The reverse was shown for the boys in the single-sex school, while for the boys in the mixed schools, nine appeared to be an age of relatively low aspirations to this particular elite. There also appeared to be a general trend among the children to desire more responsibility with increasing years, and a greater tendency to prefer the responsibilities conferred by authority (monitorial) at age eleven, than to occupy the elective office of captaincy.

On the subject of the form-captaincy, seven-year-old children rationalised these attitudes as follows:

Would you like to be a form captain? Why?

Girls' Junior School (Essex), seven-year-old girls:

YES

Because I would like to lead the class.

I would like to be a captain because I mite boss.

Liking for particular jobs.

Because you can put a team point down.

I like doing little jobs.

Because I would like to.

NO

Because you have to do things all the time.

Because everybody will come to me and it will make my work bad.

Because I do not want to.

Mixed Junior School (London), seven-year-old girls:

YES

I would be helping.

Liking for particular tasks.

Because you boss people around.

Because I would feel important.

I like to help people.

So the class would not be a mess.

So the classroom is tidy.

You are in charge of something.

NO

Because people call me Bossy Boots.

Because it is hard work.

Because I am a girl.

Because it is boy's work.

Because I do not.

Because I would not like the jobs.

Mixed Junior School (London), seven-year-old boys:

YES

I would be able to help others.

Liking for particular jobs.

Because you can put names down.

Because I can be in charge of things.

Because I wouldn't have to play.

Because nobody would boss you about.

Because they do work.

NO

Because you would work all day.

Because it is hard.

I don't like telling people what to do.

Because it might be hard work and I don't like hard work.

Would you like to be a monitor? Why?

Reactions to this followed a pattern:

Girls' Junior School (Essex), seven-year-old girls:

   YES

   Liking for 'doing jobs' was again the general reason.

   NO

   Reasons were not given beyond 'Because I do not want to'.

Mixed Junior School (London), seven-year-old girls:

   YES

   So the classroom is tidy.

   You are in charge of something.

   NO

   No, it is boring.

Mixed Junior School (London), seven-year-old boys:

   YES

   Because I could help with some jobs.

Reasons for choices corresponded between the three groups. Children showed themselves to be capable of conceptually separating 'helping', 'leading' and 'working' functions and making a personal decision as to the intrinsic or extrinsic worth of power and its instrumental value in their own situation. One boy displayed a self-knowledge and self-acceptance many adults might envy: 'Because it might be hard work and I don't like hard work!' While another hinted at thwarted ambitions: 'It is a nice job and for once you are in charge'.

Leadership concepts, and motivation to lead, can obviously exist as early as the age of seven; as also can altruism, social responsibility, ambition and self-doubt.

CHILDREN'S PERCEPTIONS OF PARLIAMENT AND MEMBERS OF PARLIAMENT

The questions 'Do you know what Parliament is? Do you know what people do there? Do you know how people come to be there?' require answers which contain specific information and showed children of consecutive ages making steady gains in the proportion of questions answered successfully. The first two show children making considerable gains at nine, and again at eleven, while the third, which is much less successfully answered throughout shows children's achievement rising most steeply at the age of ten. The conclusion here is that more is known of the activity of Parliament than of the functions of elections.

Members of Parliament are regarded as a 'special' elite. Low expectations were shown of the possibility of joining this group, the youngest children, of seven, being the most optimistic in this respect. These attitudes are also revealed in responses to the next questions. The 'cleverness' of law-makers is assessed next; all groups felt the need for 'people who make the laws to be very clever', if not more clever than most other people. Some of the reasons and descriptions children of different ages gave, in response to these questions, are quoted below.

Children's perceptions of what MPs and parliament do

Seven-year-old girls:

They make laws and biuld biuldings (sic).

Choose the govement (sic).

Group round and discuss the laws. People vote for them.

They do lots of work.

Seven-year-old boys:

They make ruls (sic).

They decide laws. They build houses.

Talk.

Eight-year-old girls:

They look after the country and make sure everybody believes in doing the law.

They make laws to keep the country under control.

Eight-year-old boys:

They help the country and try to stop strikes.

They put prices on the food.

Nine-year-old girls:

They make decisions.

They talk.

They govern the country and they lead parties.

They make laws and control the country.

They vote for people they want to be Prime Minister.

Nine-year-old boys:

Parliament is a group of men trying to help the country.

People decide if laws should be made or not.

They've been elected by other citizens.

Parliament is a place where the Prime Minister works.

They belong to a party and try to be the political member of a town.

The members of Parliament make sure the government is in order.

Members of Parliament make speeches in Whitehall.

Talks about crises and things of the present.

He (an MP) discusses what the country is to be like in the future.

They help the Queen.

It is all the politicians who run the country.

They govern the country and they lead parties.

They talk about tax and the price of food and things like that.

A Member of Parliament helps make laws.

Ten-year-old girls:

A member of Parliament is someone out of a group of people who help to run the country.

They tell us what will happen in the future.

The government are people who discuss the state of the country and help us.

The government rule the country and the Parliament make the laws.

The government is a group of intelligent people that make the laws.

They bring trouble to the Prime Minister.

They bring complaints to the Prime Minister and tell him what the people want.

They discuss Britain's affairs and what they should do.

People voted for them to be there.

Members of Parliament govern Britain and pass laws to help us.

They make the rules and keep Britain in order.

They make decisions on what they think is best for the country.

Ten-year-old boys:

There are three parties, when they win a general election they become the government.

The government makes laws.

People vote because they want a person to lead them.

They put their name in the district to a candadate (sic) and then get a lot of votes.

They get into Parliament.

To vote is to help a party.

Parliament decides wages, makes laws.

They put up pensions for old people.

They deal with current affairs.

Parliament is a place where MPs disguise matters of importance.

They make rules and represent their own parties.

Parliament is some people who talk about the government.

Eleven-year-old girls:

He (an MP) brings problems to the Prime Minister.

Both rule the country and make laws to help everyone.

The government looks after the present state of the country.

They make the rules and laws.

They are the Queens advisers.

A government is a group of people who decide what should happen to prices and things.

They are able to rule the country.

Make decisions.

The government governs the country and members of Parliament make new laws.

Parliament is a place where the MPs work and pass the laws.

People come to be there by being elected by people who think (they) are good enough to cope with the problems.

Eleven-year-old boys:

They (MPs) speak out and tell other members about their schemes to improve the country.

They get voted in by the people in their constituency.

They help the Prime Minister and they argue with the Prime Minister.

Improve our standard of living, make new laws, deal in foreign matters.

They make laws and try to settle strikes.

The government rules the country and a member of Parliament is a person that belongs to the House of Commons.

Look after the state and the nation.

They make decisions, laws like the Common Market.

CHILDREN'S ATTITUDES TO GOVERNMENT

The children questioned were found to be strongly committed to the idea of the benevolence of political figures and of the political culture generally. More required their MPs to be good than clever, and believed that this was indeed so; MPs must be, for most, at least, 'as good as' other people. There were very few subscribers to the Machiavellian ethic.

Do MPs need to be good? Do they need to be as good as other people?

Eight-year-old girls:

So they can give fair laws.

Because they might make bad laws.

Because they are ordinary people.

Because we might be unhappy and live with wicked people.

Eight-year-old boys:

Because if they're better than other people it's easy to do things and do them quick.

Because they will be lowering the country.

At this stage, the girls appeared more inclined to interpret the term 'good' morally, while boys preferred often to attach the meaning 'good at' to their responses. At nine, some girls assumed particular qualities in the elected elite.

Nine-year-old girls:

They are good already.

Because they would not be one (an MP) if they were not.

To be kind to our country.

While others took a less sentimental viewpoint, typically:

Because they have responsible jobs, and it wouldn't be very good if they were bad.

Many boys, at this age, have no charisma attached to leadership:

Nine-year-old boys:

They are just people.

Yes, they do, because they make laws and they have to keep them as well.

Yes, because you do not have to be clever to make a law.

Because if they are not, other people should get the chances.

The ten-year-olds introduced further thinking here:

Ten-year-old girls:

> Yes, because otherwise they might make silly decisions.
>
> Because they are very important.

Ten-year-old boys:

> Yes, otherwise they would make laws to suit themselves.
>
> Because they have to understand people.

And one moral philosopher reminded:

> Nobody can be as good as somebody else.

At eleven-years, a developed attitude showed for both boys and girls:

Eleven-year-old girls:

> If they wasn't good enough, they wouldn't be in Parliament.
>
> Because they understand problems and know how to deal with them.

These comments encapsulate some of the girls' willingness to project particular qualities upon leadership; 'importance' has its moral charisma, apparently, and although this is not true of all girls' responses, it is an attitude that occurred with them much more frequently than with the boys, who appeared more conscious of moral imperatives here.

Eleven-year-old boys:

> They should show an example.
>
> They have to be honest.
>
> If they weren't good, they wouldn't be leaders, because they wouldn't be good enough to be them.

The 'goodness' requirement for Members of Parliament was the strongest positive response throughout the age-range of children questioned, and across the different schools. Cleverness is not enough, according to most children; fairness demands that those who make the rules shall abide by them and be seen to be morally capable of ruling. 'If they were bad they would write bad laws,' said both a seven-year-old and a ten-year-old. It is interesting to see that even at the early age of seven the possibility of a 'bad' law is considered; at seven, the same expected tribulations appear to be attached to the possibility of bad or unfair laws as to the abolition of school rules, and for the same reasons. Security is based upon a rule-governed society, benevolently administered.

Children's basic needs include security and the minimisation of their feelings of vulnerability. For these reasons they need to project benevolent intentions and qualities upon those who govern them in day-to-day situations. This affective response is transferred to other types of authority, ultimately to government itself.

PARTIES AND PERSONALITIES

This section presents a series of further comparisons. I have related questions and compared children's ways of dealing with them at seven, nine and eleven.

What do you think politics is about?

Girls' Junior School (Essex), seven-year-old girls:

> I think politics is about making ruls.
>
> I don't know. Have something to do with Laber.
>
> I think it is about histrey.
>
> People talk with other people.

Mixed Junior School (London), seven-year-old girls:

> Science.
>
> Labour and Libral parties.
>
> Parties.

Mixed Junior School (London), seven-year-old boys:

> Voting.
>
> The priminester.
>
> Parties.
>
> It is a party.
>
> It is something about voting.

Girls' Junior School (Essex), nine-year-old girls:

> Asking people what to do.
>
> Political parties.

Voting.

Politics is about parliment.

I think it is about laws.

Prime Minister.

History.

Boys' Junior School (Essex), nine-year-old boys:

It is about Pallerment.

Trying to look after the country.

Governing the country.

Protect the country.

Money.

It is about the State of Britain.

Makeing laws.

Mixed Junior School (London), nine-year-old girls:

Doing thing(s) for the country.

I think it is about the laws of the country and the way we make and spend money.

People who belong to parties that help you.

Work to do with the Prime Minister.

Politics is about the parties.

Ruling London.

It is about who should be the next Prime Minister.

I think it is about when Conservative, Labour and Liberal disagree about something.

Mixed Junior School (London), nine-year-old boys:

They are the parties like Edward Heath.

About the wo(r)ld.

Somebody who belongs to a party to help the country.

They help the guvern.

Laws and how to keep the country.

Politics keep Britain on there feet.

Governing the country.

I think it is about the government parties.

Labour, Conservative, Libarel.

I think it (is) to help the country.

Ruling London.

The ruling of the country.

Girls' Junior School (Essex), eleven-year-old girls:

People go voteing every year.

Wages, prices and tax etc.

I think politics is about law.

Boys' Junior School (Essex), eleven-year-old boys:

About the law and the prices of food etc.

Who's going to be Priminister.

Mixed Junior School (London), eleven-year-old girls:

Ruling the country.

It is to keep the country together.

Government.

Financial problems.

Politics is about Priministers.

It is a group which stand as our country and make deals with other countries.

Helping your country.

What people think to run the country.

Keeps the country in order.

It's about a group of people fighting.

I think that unless the government does something about the country, the country is going to be in such a state that nobody will be able to cope with it.

First of all they should house people and instead of spending money on cars, building some council houses.

There should be more jobs available and everyone should help each other.

I think the government should not spend as much money on building roads and cars.

They should leave some of the country as countryside.

Mixed Junior School (London), eleven-year-old boys:

It is about the country's affairs and foreign affairs.

It is to do with government and ruling the country.

Trade unions.

It's about parties deciding.

The future of Britain, government.

I think they are about voting.

I think that politics is to keep the country going.

Order in the country and prices going up.

About money and affairs concerning the country.

It is what people think to run the country.

Making rules.

Keeping Great Britain a decent place.

The government of our country.

It is about finding out what's best for your country.

Politics is a group of different thought put together on the economy of the country.

The wealth of our country and people.

The Common Market.

Running the country.

Keeping the country in order.

What do you think political parties do?

Girls' Junior School (Essex), seven-year-old girls:

Talk about things.

Play games.

They is political.

They make laws.

Because they are people's party.

They vote.

About th lor (sic).

Mixed Junior School (London), seven-year-old girls:

Write about other people.

Vote if they want thing.

To see who will be Prime Minister.

Mixed Junior School (London), seven-year-old boys:

They vote.

They tok to gathe (talk together).

To government.

Help the Queen.

Find out if we go out of the comon market or stay in.

Girls' Junior School (Essex), nine-year-old girls:

It is where people sit and talk.

They talk about electshions.

Talk.

Talk to each other.

Political parties are election parties.

They vote.

Look after us.

They help the countrys.

Make better laws.

Boys' Junior School (Essex), nine-year-old boys:

Talk about the electoin.

They talk about what to do.

Vote against each other.

To decus.

Put prices up and down.

They make speechs at meetings.

Make laws.

Mixed Junior School (London), nine-year-old girls:

Help the country.

Help people.

To help with the country and vote.

I think that they try to do things they think is right concerning the country and the people.

They vote.

They help you.

Where the Prime Minister meets with other people.

The parties try and make people vote for them.

Discuss important things.

I think political parties argue about something.

Mixed Junior School (London), nine-year-old boys:

Vote.

They try to decide what is right.

Help us.

They deskus.

They do what they think best.

To stop crises.

Auganise things.

Help people.

I think they deal with keeping Britain going.

Look after the country.

They do things that's best for the country.

Discuss important things.

Girls' Junior School (Essex), eleven-year-old girls:

They try to choose the best for our country.

They have meetings on whether to raise or lower wages and prices.

See who is going to be Prime Minister.

Boys' Junior School (Essex), eleven-year-old boys:

Cut down prices.

Mixed Junior School (London), eleven-year-old girls:

Ruling the country.

Govern the country.

They help with all business problems, etc.

The political parties argue with other parties.

So that we get the best for our country.

Decide who is going to be Prime Minister and different things.

Talk about their own problems.

They try to get a better government.

They all have different views of the country.

Political parties fight for rights to help the country.

Mixed Junior School (London), eleven-year-old boys:

They try to help the government.

They think of ideas for the country to choose.

There to help prices not going up.

Try to get a better government.

Make rules.

Make ideas of governing the country.

They all try and make people vote their way because they think it is right.

Nothing except argue.

Have their own views of running the country.

Organise different things.

Give their own views.

They fight to gain power.

Make the country what it is.

Compete against each other.

Have different views about keeping the country in order.

Why do we have different parties?

Girls' Junior School (Essex), seven-year-old girls:

Becose there are different names.

Becaese of all sorts of things.

We have different parties so that there is Labour.

To talk about things.

Beycos it is in difrun plasis (sic).

Because every party does a different thing.

Because of Laber and Librall.

They tell us about histrey.

Otherwise we get bored.

Mixed Junior School (London), seven-year-old girls:

So that we can vote.

Because Prime Minister ned a teme (sic).

Mixed Junior School (London), seven-year-old boys:

So that one person doesn't have to be Prime Minister all the time.

Because otherwise we would have everything the same.

People like different people.

Girls' Junior School (Essex), nine-year-old girls:

We have different parties to look after us.

To think about uffer (other) people.

To do a lot of work.

So we can vote.

Because they are not all the same.

Because they are many man (men).

To see which man is going to be Prime Minister.

Because if it was all one party it would be too big.

We have different parties because some parties are big and small.

Because they have different meetings.

We have different parties because we no all about election.

I think we have different parties to help us.

We have different parties for voting.

To vote for different people.

So we can vote for them.

So that we have a choice of people to look after the country.

We have different parties so that we have a Priminster each.

So that we don't get mixed up.

Boys' Junior School (Essex), nine-year-old boys:

Because people might not like one party.

To help the country.

Because when we vote one comes throgh.

If we have the same parties it will be boring each year.

Because they want different Prime Ministers.

For elections.

Because we would get fed up with the same one.

Because we would get fed up with the same Prime Minister.

To compeet again ech over.

So we can have different Prime Ministers.

Mixed Junior School (London), nine-year-old girls:

So they won't always agreed the same thing.

To see who wins.

We have different parties so that we can decide how we want to govern.

To vote for the Priminester.

Because they work for different things.

To see if other parties have better suggestions.

So that (a) party is not a government all the time.

Because they all have different ideas.

So we can vote.

So people who think parties are right can choose which is right.

We have different parties because if we just had one person we wouldn't have anybody chosen for Prime Minister.

Mixed Junior School (London), nine-year-old boys:

Because we want different leaders.

To vote against each other.

So if one is bad we get a new one.

We are different parties.

Because they think differently.

To have competitions.

So each time we don't get a different government.

Because some have different schemes.

So we can vote for different people.

Girls' Junior School (Essex), eleven-year-old girls:

They try to choose the law for our country.

Because some poor people like a working party and rich people like to have their own party.

Who will be Prime Minister.

Boys' Junior School (Essex), eleven-year-old boys:

So we can. for the that think are the best (sic).

Mixed Junior School (London), eleven-year-old girls:

To get different opinions.

Because people may want to vote different.

So we can change instead of having the same one.

Because each party has a different point of view.

To figure out difficult things.

To argue.

Because we all have different views on different things.

To give us a choice.

To talk about different politics.

Because if you had the same party they would not have as many ideas or may not be good at ruling.

Mixed Junior School (London), eleven-year-old boys:

Because different people agree on different things.

Each party does different things.

Some might be better.

So there are different views.

Because one wants to win.

One group of people agree about one thing and another group agrees on another thing.

Because we can vote different.

To choose the one picked to rule the country.

Because different parties stand for different things.

So we can choose which has the best policies.

Get different decisions.

Otherwise we would have the same ideas.

To fight for rights for different grades of people.

Better deals and new Prime Minister.

So people have a choice of views.

Some parties are bad.

People believe in different things.

So that they can come to a firm agreement.

Do you think the different parties agree about most things?

Girls' Junior School (Essex), seven-year-old girls:
Yes: 20 (62%)   No: 6 (19%)   Don't know: 6 (19%)

Mixed Junior School (London), seven-year-old girls:
Yes: 2 (14%)   No: 3 (21%)   Don't know: 9 (65%)

Mixed Junior School (London), seven-year-old boys:
Yes: 3 (20%)   No: 4 (27%)   Don't know: 8 (53%)

Girls' Junior School (Essex), nine-year-old girls:
Yes: 28 (52%)   No: 12 (22%)   Don't know: 14 (26%)

Boys' Junior School (Essex), nine-year-old boys:
Yes: 4 (16%)   No: 9 (36%)   Don't know: 12 (48%)

Mixed Junior School (London), nine-year-old girls:
Yes: 5 (45%)   No: 5 (45%)   Don't know: 1 (10%)

Mixed Junior School (London), nine-year-old boys:
Yes: 4 (29%)   No: 8 (57%)   Sometimes: 2 (14%)   Don't know: 0

Girls' Junior School (Essex), eleven-year-old girls:
Yes: 1 (33%)   No: 2 (67%)   Don't know: 0

Boys' Junior School (Essex), eleven-year-old boys:
Yes: 0   No: 2 (100%)   Don't know: 0

(From one boy: No, because otherwise we would have a national crisis.)

Mixed Junior School (London), eleven-year-old girls:
Yes: 5 (26%)   No: 10 (53%)   Don't know: 4 (21%)

Mixed Junior School (London), eleven-year-old-boys:
Yes: 6 (21%)   No: 19 (65%)   Sometimes: 2 (7%)   Don't know: 2 (7%)

What kind of things might they not agree about?

Girls' Junior School (Essex), seven-year-old girls:
Who is going to be Prime Minister.
Being someone.
Prices.
Ivorys thing (everything).
They might not agree about god.

Mixed Junior School (London), seven-year-old girls:
Things going up.
Do not have enuf money.
Being part of Eupeen.

Mixed Junior School (London), seven-year-old boys:
Who should be Prime Minister.
People being in palement.
London Bridge was to open every hour.
Who is Prime Minister.
Staying in or out of the Common Market.

Girls' Junior School (Essex), nine-year-old girls:
Most things.
They do not agree about conncel (sic).
People running on football grounds.
They might not agree about politics.
Prices.
Like chuking Wilson out of his job.
Elections.
They might not agree with executing murderes.
They don't agree about nothing apart from elections.
About different Labour.
They might not agree about the votes what people give in.

Giving people more money.

How to run the country.

A man might say someone is a good leader somebody else might not.

About some laws.

Doing work.

Building home.

About food going up.

They might not agree about giving rises.

Boys' Junior School (Essex), nine-year-old boys:

Changing all the laws in England.

Throwing bombs.

Having anover Prime Minister.

Mr Heath.

Talking about who should come thour.

The prices of things.

About who will be Priminster.

Some laws.

Prices pentions rents.

About food and pensions and rates.

Mixed Junior School (London), nine-year-old girls:

Buildings.

Flowers.

Voting each other's parties.

About how to govern country and who governs it.

The Priminester.

Getting out of the Common Market.

Having extra supermarkets.

What people do.

Wages and inflation.

A person to be Prime Minister.

They might not agree about whose the next Prime Minister.

About prices of things.

Mixed Junior School (London), nine-year-old boys:

Who is Prime Minister.

Fuel crisis.

Building houses.

Prices.

Housing.

Keeping Britain out of Europe and elections.

Holding banners, etc.

Income tax, mortgages, etc.

Prices of food.

They might not agree about things that we get from other countries.

How to look after the country.

Money.

Girls' Junior School (Essex), eleven-year-old girls:

Wages, prices, elections, morgiges, tax, new laws.

Who's going to be Prime Minister.

Boys' Junior School (Essex), eleven-year-old boys:

The growing prices on food.

Who should be Priminister.

Mixed Junior School (London), eleven-year-old girls:

Electing someone.

Food prices and things like that.

Who should be Prime Minister.

Electing a Prime Minister.

About who can rule the country.

Schools, about comprehensive schools.

Prices of things.

Deals with other countries.

About who's going to knock those houses down and mostly everything.

Who is going to lead.

Food prices, petrol, etc.

About prices and inflation.

Voting.

They do not agree about being in the Common Market or not.

Mixed Junior School (London), eleven-year-old boys:

About how much wage people should get.

Wage packet, food prices, inflation.

Who should win the elections.

Prices of food, etc.

Prices, inflation.

Taxes and rules.

Taxes, schools.

Who's going to be Prime Minister.

Equality.

How to fight inflation and things such as that.

Common Market.

Inflation, Common Market, Food.

Who should govern the country.

Wages, inflation.

What does the Prime Minister do?

Girls' Junior School (Essex), seven-year-old girls:

He signs important papers.

The Prime Minister look after the connortay.

I think he rules the conutrey.

He helps people.

He tells us the news.

He is on teley.

The Prime Ministers the Govment.

I think he makes prices higher.

He voters.

He tavles round weld.

He looks after our country.

He signs letters.

He does the noes (news).

He tells all about the world.

He is a Prinse and woks for the aremy.

Mixed Junior School (London), seven-year-old girls:

He plays golf.

Leader.

He works on papays.

He goes to important meetings.

He does work.

News.

He tells people to bluid houses.

He goes to very important meetings.

He puts prises on shop things.

He send people to gaol.

He makes peace.

He juges.

He writes letters.

Writes about things.

He talks to the MPs.

He tells us the rules.

He wrights things for the Queen.

Tell you what to do.

Mixed Junior School (London), seven-year-old boys:

He goes to very important meetings and says his speech.

He works with the govermant.

Opens letters.

He sometimes torks with orther people.

He tell people to do thin(g)s.

He writes letters.

He rules ingland.

Makes things go up.

He talks to the MPs.

He rules over the country.

He does some writhing (sic).

Judges.

Writes letters.

He helps in the budget and finds out about the voting.

He works but has some rest.

Girls' Junior School (Essex), nine-year-old girls:

He puts food prices up.

Elections and speeches.

Looks after the government.

Rules his part of the country.

He is on television.

He pays the wages to the men who work.

He keeps his eye on the prises.

Making sure that everything is right for the people.

Helps the Queen rule the world.

He rules the country.

He looks after all the country and talks about money, tax, etc.

He has meetings and talks to other people.

He forms a government; he enters and withdraws us from the Common Market.

He works out problems of the world.

Works in Parliament.

Boys' Junior School (Essex), nine-year-old boys:

Looks after the country.

In charge of rent and wages.

Rules the workers.

Leads the country.

A lot of talking about Labour and Conservatives.

He keeps the country carm (sic) and he looks after the world.

He does elections.

Mixed Junior School (London), nine-year-old girls:

I think he makes final decisions and governs England.

He leads the government of parliament.

He tells us to put prices up or down.

Looks after people.

He does things about things going wrong.

In charge of meetings.

In charge of a comitey.

I think the PM settles things.

Gives orders to people.

Mixed Junior School (London), nine-year-old boys:

He talks to other Prime Ministers.

Works in the Houses of Parliament.

Discusses political matters.

Travels around.

He makes the laws.

He works in politics.

Rules the government.

Talks with Unions.

He tries to control inflation.

He auganises political parties and he is the head of the Labour Party.

He decides if laws are fair.

Mixed Junior School (Kent), nine-year-old girls:

Looks after the country.

He does the rules for things and tells you what to do if you don't know.

Signs papers all the time and talks.

He helps the Queen.

He helps the people.

Does speeches.

Mixed Junior School (Kent), nine-year-old boys:

Talks to foring (sic) ministers.

Helps people.

Makes rules.

He goes around the country seeing how they are getting on.

When he goes to see the Queen he tells the Queen something.

Works for GB to keep their power cuts and saves it for Christmas.

Girls' Junior School (Essex), eleven-year-old girls:

He puts up prices and gives people wages and pensions, and puts mortgages on houses.

He does the prices and government.

Boys' Junior School (Essex), eleven-year-old boys:

Cuts inflation. Puts tax on things. He tries to make respect to law.

He cuts or stops the prices of everything going up.

Looks after the land.

He keeps England at peace.

Mixed Junior School (London), eleven-year-old girls:

He keeps the country in order, and he keeps Parliament in order.

Goes to conferences and makes speeches.

He is the Queen's adviser, keeps the country in order and makes the law.

Mixed Junior School (Kent), eleven-year-old boys:

Looks after the place.

Keeps the country in order and makes decisions.

He does most of the work for our country.

He tries to stop strikes.

Mixed Junior School (Kent), eleven-year-old girls:

He travels a lot and he is an MP.

He rules the country.

He helps the countries in the Common Market.

Looks after the country and joins us in the Common Market with other countries to trade.

Looks after our country.

He helps the country to keep the rules and to keep you from danger.

Mixed Junior School (Kent), eleven-year-old boys:

I think he puts up prices and sends more plastic things abroad.

Tries to keep all of the prices down so we can spend less money and he tries to get some more oil into England.

He makes the laws of the land.

He makes the rules we live by.

He solves the country's problems.

He tries to keep the prices down, and he looks after the state of the country.

Not very much at all.

Sits in his office all day and thinks about conferences.

What kind of things should a Prime Minister do?

Girls' Junior School (Essex), seven-year-old girls:

The Prime Minister should look af(ter) the country.

He should make evrey body happy.

Help people and do things for people.

Make good rooles.

Say the news.

Has tu dow wuc (sic).

Work hard and writ a lote.

I think he should not put prices higher.

Give medals.

The Prime Minister should look after the pepple.

Do ruls.

He should look after our contrey.

Tell us news that's what he should do.

Make laws.

Mixed Junior School (London), seven-year-old girls:

Help people.

Write about things and about people.

Tell people to pay taxs.

He should give fair price on things.

Give more money to the workers.

Mixed Junior School (London), seven-year-old boys:

Good things.

Make good rules.

Look after the country.

Writing and work.

Good work.

Find out about the voting.

Girls' Junior School (Essex), nine-year-old girls:

Put prices down.

Take prices down from food.

Sort things out.

Tell people to be kind and good.

Work a lot.

Make the prices go up.

He should make laws.

He should talk about things.

The Prime Minister should stop things.

Speeches.

A Prime Minister should look after the country.

Help people a lot.

Say things on TV.

A Prime Minister should pay wages to the workers.

A Prime Minister should take care of politics.

Stop people having wars.

Make things cheaper and take away tax and give more. wages for those who don't earn much.

Do good things.

Save Briton.

Form a sensible government.

Tell the truth.

Put down the price of food.

Not boss people about and make people go on strike.

Rule the country.

Boys' Junior School (Essex), nine-year-old boys:

Look after his country.

Work.

Help people.

Help the country.

He should look after the law.

Put the prices down and allso don't give oil away.

Reduse the prices of food/of things.

Put down prices.

Make laws.

Lead the country.

Mixed Junior School (London), nine-year-old girls:

Do thing(s) for the country.

Good things.

He should try to give Britain a better place in the world and do what is right.

He should look after the government.

He should tell us what happens throughout the country.

Look after his country and see that items aren't dear.

He should explain things that are new.

Discuss matters and help.

He should try to stop people fighting.

He should make decisions.

Mixed Junior School (London), nine-year-old boys:

Not put the prices up.

He should be Prime Minister of a town.

Send prices up or down.

Look after houses.

Keep the country's prices low as possible.

Control Britain.

Be honest and keeping the law.

Help the country.

Make the old peoples pensions higher.

He might let communism in.

Make changes in the country.

Girls' Junior School (Essex), eleven-year-old girls:

He should decide about prices and government.

He should try to help poor people.

He would put prices up on food.

Boys' Junior School (Essex), eleven-year-old boys:

Cut inflation.

Keep laws.

Mixed Junior School (London), eleven-year-old girls:

Think of people now himself.

Help keep prices down.

See that the country is in order.

Look after the country.

A Prime Minister should rule the country.

Get the best for us.

Settle arguments of all sorts.

Put up more shops and houses where needed.

Rule the government wisely.

He should try to get people on his side.

Help us with all the things.

A Prime Minister should help his people.

Mixed Junior School (London), eleven-year-old boys:

He should make sure prices stay at a steady price.

Think of the elderly and poor.

Try to stop trade increase.

He should help decide on an agreement.

Keep the boys and girls quiet.

Help the welf (sic) of the country.

Help the country as it goes.

Try and keep inflation down.

Make the prices of food stand at a level.

He thinks of others.

Freeze prices.

Stop inflation from getting worse.

Improve on what is already done.

Make England a better place.

He for one should try to keep prices down and prevent unemployment.

Make speeches.

Make country more powerful.

Develop the country's state to a good state.

Give more money to people.

Keep inflation down.

Keep wages sensible.

How does a Prime Minister decide what to do?

Girls' Junior School (Essex), seven-year-old girls:

He thinks.

Bi going to metins (sic)

By thinking very hard.

Mixed Junior School (London), seven-year-old girls:

He thinks.

By thinking.

People help him.

By asking people what they would do if they would do.

Mixed Junior School (London), seven-year-old boys:

He votes.

By thinking.

He decides with men.

Political party tells him.

By the queen orders.

Girls' Junior School (Essex), nine-year-old girls:

With help from his party.

He writes letters to the concil.

He tells a lot of other people.

With help from the parties.

He has a meeting with other members.

He has a meeting with other people.

He things.

He has meetings and talks.

He decides what to do by reading (the) paper.

He votes.

He put it to the vote.

He has people who help him.

He tells the other people.

He makes laws that other people approve of.

He calls a meeting.

By having a talk with other Prime Minister.

His party helps him decide.

Boys' Junior School (Essex), nine-year-old boys:

He has been told.

He votes.

He ask Mr Heath.

Ask other people.

He asks the rest of the party.

He asks.

Have meetings.

He forms meetings.

Let people vote.

Mixed Junior School (London), nine-year-old girls:

He decide(s) because people help him.

He thinks it over.

He decides by asking the people and having meetings.

He thinks hard.

By looking (at) what is happening.

By having different votes.

By making speeches.

He calls on his fellow-partners.

He decides what to do because he has to.

Mixed Junior School (London), nine-year-old boys:

He thinks.

He votes.

By help.

He gathers up people.

He asks the nation.

Goes (to) cabinet for some information.

By deciding which is wrong and right.

By having elections.

He decides what to do by having a conference.

The Queen tells him.

He does not, he gets help.

He has a meeting to decide.

By the partys.

Girls' Junior School (Essex), eleven-year-old girls:

He decides with his party and then he knows what to do.

By having meeting with other important people.

He thinks what to do.

Boys' Junior School (Essex), eleven-year-old boys:

He have a meeting with the parties.

Mixed Junior School (London), eleven-year-old girls:

Asks the Queen, he has a party political broadcast.

He decides with his ministers.

Talks with his party.

From the help of the rest of Parliament.

By elections.

He gives the suggestion to the cabinet and find(s) they hink out what.

He has meetings with his parties.

Well, he first of all decides what to do with his government.

Mixed Junior School (London), eleven-year-old boys:

Have a ballot and asks fellow MPs.

He decides by communicating with other politicians.

He thinks and does his best to do it.

See what other(s) think.

By the help of his Minister.

He asks the other politicians.

He has a meeting with his Party to agree.

By talking with his men at Parliament.

Asks his advisers.

By help of MPs.

By the country's votes.

Thinks on all possibilities.

He figures out how to fight things, and how to get the best things for his country.

With his brains.

On what the other members of the party say.

He asks different people.

He consults his ministers.

He asks for votes from those in his party.

He is told what to do.

By sorting out the matter with the government.

Have meetings.

What does the Queen do that you know about?

Girls' Junior School (Essex), seven-year-old girls:

The Queen sits on a thrown.

No, I do not think the Queen does any work.

She helps people.

She writes letters.

She calls a servant.

She rites things on paper and goes to other countries.

She rids a horse.

She goes round the world.

She gives medals out.

Mixed Junior School (London), seven-year-old girls:

She looks after the palace.

She rules the country.

Meets people.

Housework, meets people.

She reads papers from people.

She gose trouping.

She tells people what to do.

She reads papers from people.

She wears Juals.

She travels to look after people.

Looks after the Kingdom.

She rules.

She talks.

She writes letters to people who are a hundred.

She tells the government.

Offes (sic) work.

She does a parade.

Mixed Junior School (London), seven-year-old boys:

She goes to trouping of the colour and receives the new colour.

Rules the country.

Visits places.

She does work.

She reads speeches.

She does messegs.

She helps to rule two countries, Australia and England.

Goes to another country.

She goes to parts of GB.

Writes letters and rule the country.

She helps the mayor.

She visits different places at different times.

Girls' Junior School (Essex), nine-year-old girls:

The Queen helps us to do nearly everything.

The Queen visits different countries.

Speeches.

Rules the country.

Writes things and goes to football matches.

She looks after England.

The Queen rides about in a carriage and waves.

Goes to dances.

She goes round the world talking to help people.

She lives in a big house and rules.

She cristhens ships and opens buildings.

Makes speeches for us.

She goes to different countries and talks to Prime Ministers, and on television.

She helps to keep the country in order, she helps the pensioners.

Boys' Junior School (Essex), nine-year-old boys:

Visits countrys.

Gives soldiers medals.

Goes to weddings.

Travels around the world.

Talks about the House of Lords.

Makes speeches.

Horse-riding.

Governs Britain.

She goes in coaches.

Mixed Junior School (London), nine-year-old girls:

She rules the country and tries to do as much for the people as she can.

Fills in forms and papers.

She names ships.

Travels to many countries.

Rules her country.

Opens many things.

Writes letters to people answering their letters.

Rule the kingdom.

Mixed Junior School (London), nine-year-old boys:

She works on the oil.

Paper work.

Visits places.

Visits people, goes to talks, gives medals.

She signs many documents and writes letters.

Rules the country and governs things.

She gets all we need.

She goes to any celebration.

Gives advice to the Prime Minister.

She makes laws.

All I know is that she reigns Britain .

Mixed Junior School (Kent), nine-year-old girls:

Visits other countries.

She has to sign things.

Goes to meetings to help the people.

Mixed Junior School (Kent), nine-year-old boys:

Go to countries.

Paper work.

Rules the Country.

Shakes hands with a lot of people.

Looks after England.

She writes letters to ambassadors in other countries.

Girls' Junior School (Essex), eleven-year-old girls:

The Queen goes to other countries, and writes letters to people.

She helps people who are poor and she helps the government and deals with strikes. She goes to many places but she doesn't have to pay.

Boys' Junior School (Essex), eleven-year-old boys:

She opens famous buildings.

She goes on a lot of cruises.

She looks after the land.

Goes to events and tournaments.

Mixed Junior School (London), eleven-year-old girls:

She helps in Parliament.

She goes to different countries.

She works in the office at Buckingham Palace.

Mixed Junior School (London), eleven-year-old boys:

Looks after the country.

She is head of Gt Britain.

She helps.

She rules the country and deals with foreign affairs.

Mixed Junior School (Kent), eleven-year-old girls:

The Queen rules a lot of countries, and I bet that is a hard job to do.

Helps rule the country.

The Queen rules England.

Makes friends with different countries.

Rules the world.

She rules the country to try to help us.

Mixed Junior School (Kent), eleven-year-old boys:

I think she tries to keep the peace.

The Queen does all letters from other Prime Ministers and other lands.

Visits other countries.

She feeds her corgi dogs.

She rules the country.

She visits other countries to show friendship.

The Queen helps the country.

Work in an office of her own and gets served when it is meal times.

Do you know what the House of Commons and the House of Lords are?

Girls' Junior School (Essex), seven-year-old girls:

The House of Lords – that is all Lords.

In the House of Commons they have meetings.

The House of Lords is when you go to Church or Sunday School.

It is a plase waer you can make lors (sic).

Mixed Junior School (London), seven-year-old girls:

The House of Commons is in London.

Mixed Junior School (London), seven-year-old boys:

They are both Members of Parliament.

The Queen lives in it.

Girls' Junior School (Essex), nine-year-old girls:

The House of Lords is where people work.

The House of Commons is where the men have meetings.

The House of Lords important men have special meetings there.

The House of Commons is about the Prime Ministers.

Something to do with the commons market.

Where the Prime Minister go to do work.

It is royle.

The House of Commons is Big Ben and the other buildings around it.

The House of lords is were the Prime Minister lives.

Boys' Junior School (Essex), nine-year-old boys:

They are Houses of Parliament.

Mixed Junior School (London), nine-year-old girls:

Yes, the House of Commons is where they sometimes decide things.

The House of Lords is where they meet and think about different problems.

The House of Commons is where the Prime Minister decides about things.

The House of Lords is a place where all Prime Ministers meet.

The House of Commons is where they de(b)ate.

They are historical and many important talks have taken place there.

They are big buildings.

The House of Commons is where the Priministers meet.

The House of Lords is where all the important people live.

Mixed Junior School (London), nine-year-old boys:

The House of Commons is where the Prime Minister lives.

The House of Commons is a place where the Prime Minister talks.

The House holds meetings where important people go.

The House of Commons is where laws are made.

The House of Commons is where they have conferences about politics and the House of Lords is where lords meet.

The House of Commons is where the Prime Ministers meet.

Girls' Junior School (Essex), eleven-year-old girls:

They work at the House of Commons.

The House of Lords is where the queen's men work.

Boys' Junior School (Essex), eleven-year-old boys:

The house of commons is a place where people have meetings.

They are near the river thames near big ben.

Mixed Junior School (London), eleven-year-old girls:

They are where very special things take place.

Where government parties work.

The House of Commons is about the political parties.

The House of Commons is where all of Parliament meet and discuss.

The Commons is where the government meet and the Lords is where the Lords meet.

The House of Commons is where political people.

The House of Lords is a cour(t).

Places where rulers meet.

The House of Commons is where they have the talking.

The House of Commons is where the politic parties meet.

Well a House of Commons is where all the parties meet and discuss things and a House of Lords is similar.

Mixed Junior School (London), eleven-year-old boys:

It is where the government meet and have debates.

The House of Commons is where the common people government has meetings, the House of Lords is where the leaders of parties decide on what to do.

The House of Commons is where common people decide, the House of Lords is where Lords decide.

The House of Commons is the politicians.

The House of Commons are a lot of Minister(s).

The House of Commons is by Big Ben and the House of Lords is near where my Mum works.

Where all the politicians gather and talk.

The House of Commons is where Parliament is held where common people decide about the country. And the House of Lords is where the Lords decide.

The House of Commons is where the MPs meet.

I think it is a place for different parties.

MPs meet in House of Parliament.

It is a place where the Prime Minister and MPs and the Government meet to make important decisions about Great Britain .

They are the only houses the Queen can go in.

Sometimes politicians meet there and discuss certain things.

The House of Lords is where the retired politicians go.

Commons is where the politicians work, House of Lords is where all the ceremonial occasions.

They are very old buildings.

The House of Lords is for MPs retiring from the House of Commons.

All I know is they are situated by the Thames.

Debates can be held in both of them.

The House of Commons is a place where England's affairs are sorted out.

CHILDREN'S POLITICAL LANGUAGE

Coming across phrases such as 'I'd like to make the world ... more civil in its rights', from an eleven-year-old has the effect, at least, of making an adult reader pause, read it again, and then mentally re-arrange the words so as to give the sentence its 'proper' meaning, when a few extra words are added. Surely, we might say, the child is trying here to say something about 'civil rights' that he's not able to make clear? But it's possible that a niggling doubt could remain, especially after reading the ways in which children were usually able to communicate exactly what they meant when talking, or writing, about politics. So it is possible that this child is saying exactly what he means, and using words purposefully, to construct meaning, as he would use a tool to carry out a practical purpose. And if so, he is working with ideas and implications of a complexity that is, to say the least, surprising. Moments such as this occurred with children of all ages. And so there is a problem, of whether language was being used intentionally, or words merely uttered as some kind of reflex, unsupported by personal thinking. So it seems appropriate at this point to take a closer look at the words the children used to talk or write about politics, and try to evaluate what was happening.

From the start, children themselves introduced some basic political terms into both conversation and written responses. 'Leader', 'parties', 'making laws', 'voted in', 'voted out', 'govern', 'discuss', 'elect' were used fluently by the younger children, and the most frequent verbs to emerge at this stage were 'help', 'look after', 'talk', 'write', and 'win', which for these children seemed to summarise political activity. Political vocabulary appears to begin with single nouns or verbs, to which an appropriate qualification for categorising is soon attached. 'Rules', for example, in answer to the question of what a Prime Minister does, soon develops to 'make rules' or 'rules our country'. The idea of ruling is at this stage an extension of 'helping'.

There is perception of what might be included in ruling, rather than the concept of what it is to rule, and temporarily, it seems that an increase in understanding takes the form of adding to the list of what is ruled.

At seven, most children had some concept in broad and general terms, of the roles of Prime Minister and Monarch. These are seen as 'helping', benevolent figures, giving mostly unspecified 'help' to country, Parliament, each other and 'us', and ideas about them were constructed from these words plus a few others, such as the names of the political parties. The two most commonly used verbs, 'helping' and 'looking after', were worked very hard by children in a political context, and although the majority gradually discarded them in favour of more specific and differentiated language, some at eleven were still using 'help' and 'look after' to describe political activity.

By about eight years of age there had been decided progress for many children, who were using political phrases with accuracy. By nine, they were not only aware of voting, but also of its organisation and purposes. Governments do not simply exist, they are 'formed', and by ten years of age some children could differentiate between Government and Parliament, and understand that present issues under public discussion have both a past history and objectives located in the future. As early as nine, it appears that children relate to the 'out-there' political world and can focus on its different aspects; they are aware of negotiating activities, of 'crises' and of inflation that needs to be 'curbed' or 'brought under control'. The country is 'organised' and 'controlled', and the 'state of the country' – often '*our*' country being emphasised – is an object of concern. But the nine-year-olds used phrases that also showed wider concerns. They were in no way insular; 'problems of the world' were acknowledged as was the relationship with 'Europe' and 'the Common Market'. Some of the expressions used by this age-group revealed particular kinds of expectations, for example of their Members of Parliament, who must be 'responsible' and 'loyal'.

The material collected shows children's acquisition of political vocabulary and ideas making rapid gains between the ages of about nine and ten. By this time much of the vocabulary is well assimilated, and can be used to organise everyday speech into political meanings. This seems also to apply to ideas, so that the political 'angle' of issues or events is accepted, as was shown in one group's discussion of education, and another's of care for the environment.

As children acquire a political vocabulary, political imagination develops, and with it the urge to find language for expressing ideas. By the age of nine, much of the political language of adult life has been acquired. By eleven, many children have as good a working vocabulary for politics as many adults could claim, and a framework of ideas which, even if developed no further, will enable them to grasp the facts of current affairs, understand something of relationships between principles and issues in politics, and make their choices at general elections.

5

Children's understanding of politics

If we are to evaluate some of the factors which affect children's political ideas, we must first consider the nature of their achievements at different ages and the stages in their thinking. So it seems useful, at this point, to present a brief summary of what the children who took part in the study were able to do.

The seven-year-olds revealed thinking that was intuitive and symbolic, and ideas that were discrete and unstructured. However, it also appears that, by this stage, they have made cognitive contact with the political world, and that some have achieved, in terms of information, awareness, interest and working vocabulary, a conceptual base from which further development can take place. In the mixed group, the boys dominated the discussion and the girls accepted this.

At eight years old, children showed greater competence in using language to describe political events and made more attempts to do this. A longer concentration span was in evidence, as were improved memory functions. Thinking was intuitive and revealed awareness of relationships which the children were unable, as yet, to understand. There was some effective description of election campaigns which gave the opportunity to use political vocabulary. As with the seven-year-olds, the boys of the mixed group took the lead in discussion.

The nine-year-old group was characterised by the balanced nature of their discussion, which contributed very much to its pace. As topics changed, all the children were able to focus their attention on the new aspect of discussion, thus reinforcing interest. There were stronger members of the group, but no persistent dominance by the boys, as had occurred in the younger mixed groups. There was evidence, from some children, of strong commitment to social ideals.

During and after the nine-year-old stage, the quality of interaction in discussion was sound, giving a mature flavour of reasoned discussion to what was being said. Differences in cognitive styles were very apparent, as were differences in range of perception, the more subjective material being used by the girls, which illustrated to some extent the wide interpretations of the concepts we describe as 'political'.

The ten-year-old children were moving away from the nine-year-olds' interest in speculation and extended examples, to an awareness of reality, and attempts to relate to it. Some children made judgements on a basis of consistently held views, and there appeared to be some evaluation taking place of what was relevant to the subject under discussion. Individual styles of discussion were more in evidence, and also greater variations in motivation and willingness to articulate ideas.

Finally, the eleven-year-old stage represents considerable achievement in the development of political concepts. Further linguistic development gave an ease and confidence to discussion; competence in using political concepts extended to fluency of ideas. The ability to relate sets of ideas led to the linking of politics not only with roles, structures and policies, but with topics such as conservation, women's rights and an economic re-organisation of the country. Cognitive contact had been made not only with the political world but with other questions that were understood to be open to analysis. Questions basic to democratic processes were accepted for discussion, and the political knowledge children had in their possession was, to some extent, articulated. The concept of accountability of government was one such area, linked with a strong sense of the moral imperatives laid upon government.

Children were required, in their written responses, to present information, give some kind of judgement, or produce a reason for their 'Yes' or 'No'. Asking children for information also serves to present ideas to them; the interaction is not a static 'exchange' situation, but has a dynamic element, a possibility for growth. For example, asking children whether they know the Prime Minister's name introduces the ideas of, firstly, the existence of the political role as distinct from its successive occupants, and secondly, of institutionalised, as against personal power. That children should be able to develop such understanding by a transfer of concepts from their immediate experience appears logical, and hardly surprising. The next stage in thinking about politics is the perception of structure, and the key to this is the awareness of certain roles, and of relationships between them.

The intention of asking children to explain what the Prime Minister and the Queen actually do, was firstly that they should organise any information they have into these two categories of activities and secondly, that these categories would then become usable in children's future thinking on politics, by enabling them to form ideas of what is appropriate behaviour.

The changing style of written responses to the questions, from children between the ages of seven and eleven, illustrates some aspects of cognitive growth in politics, which can be usefully described in Piagetian terms.

COHERENCE OF THE COLLECTED DATA
WITH PIAGETIAN THEORY

Piaget's model describes certain characteristics of children's thinking during the 'intuitive' stage and the 'concrete operational' stage. For example, children at the 'intuitive' stage (approximately four to seven years old):

(1) cannot make comparisons mentally;
(2) can attend to only one aspect of an object (or person) at a time, so may adopt contradictory opinions successively;
(3) cannot imagine an ordered sequence of events, and so will use juxtaposition and arbitrary mixtures of ideas;
(4) cannot compensate relations, or see relations between relations;
(5) think egocentrically – to differentiate between their own feelings and imposed rules presents difficulties;
(6) conceive of rules as absolute and permanent.

This provides a recognisable account of the kind of responses, written and verbal, obtained from a number of the seven-year-olds.

The limitations of their thinking became obvious when children were asked to describe their conception of the Queen's activities. The ways in which they approached this problem revealed the ability to use limited knowledge, and to relate it to perceived general laws. The youngest children's contribution, 'The Queen does housework', attempted a logical premise. In the absence of any particular information, they turned to classification: the Queen is a woman; women do housework; therefore the Queen does housework. This is an operation different from basic observation such as 'she rides in a carriage', or 'she goes to a football match', where recall of a remembered image is the basic mental act. The intuitive 'she helps us' is an attempt to classify by function. Children in an intuitive stage of thinking are unable to break this down into specific 'helping' functions, because they are unable to see the relationships between first the sub-classes, and second, the related classes, for example, the needs for which such help might be required.

Development from this level, in Piaget's terms, involves progress to 'concrete-operational' thought. At this stage, children will understand:

(1) that two distinct classes of activity may be combined into a single class. For example, in politics, they will become able to use terms such as 'rule', 'govern' or 'help', as classifications for other activities, which can be specified;

(2) that changes are reversible (in other words, two classes combined, can be separated). In politics, children will become able to understand changes in government, that laws can be changed and some role-occupants replaced;

(3) that results can be obtained in different ways. Children begin to understand that adjustments of prices *or* incomes can lead to a particular result;

(4) ideas of proportionality, or relations between relations. Children become able then to discuss ideas of conflicts of rights, degrees of obligation, and the possibility of different types of social organisation;

(5) the principle of conservation (of a given amount of a substance remaining constant, although its appearance, shape, and so on, can be caused to change). This kind of understanding is linked with (2) above and enables certain kinds of political understanding to take shape, connected with the relationships between stability and change. For example, a party could have 'too strong a left wing' (in one child's words) but this could be temporary, and the party remain stable.

On this basis it is possible to understand what is happening, cognitively, when at different stages in their development of political concepts, children are able to perceive:

(1) the existence of an idea to which is attached a certain name;
(2) one aspect of the idea;
(3) that the idea has more than one aspect and that different emphases and interpretations of it are possible;
(4) that certain results accrue from acting on the basis of particular emphases or interpretations of the idea;
(5) that some results are considered by some people as more desirable than others, and the reasons for these preferences.

On this analysis there is a 'family resemblance' between political and moral concepts, and the ways in which their meanings can be grasped and developed by children. For Piaget, the development of moral rationality is the same stage-by-stage process through which rationality in general develops. It proceeds by the interaction of thought and experience, based upon children's relationships with their peers and with adults. The first morality, that of constraint, is replaced eventually by that of co-operation.

The children's responses to questions concerning support for rules reveals a strong support for a morality of constraint, or a readiness to rationalise this support. This was done intuitively at first, in terms of vague fears of a state of chaos which was only kept at bay by the rules of school. With development, morality was in terms of co-operation within the school, and the desire for the school to present a good image to the world. Children were willing to promote the common interests and preferred, generally, to do this as team-work rather than be given personal authority or power. For some of the older children, a rational morality was projected on to the world at large, in the assumption that people will act on 'right reasons' when these are known.

The differences in the moral outlook of the children involved in the study, at different ages, can also be expressed in terms of the stages used by Kohlberg (1971). The morality of conventional role-conformity, in which children desire approval from others, and act in 'authority-maintaining' ways, was strongly in evidence, although some older children showed a more developed awareness, in understanding the possibility of moral choices.

Evidence for these stages was drawn from the conversations with children, and their written responses concerning the 'goodness' of ruling groups. Moral imperatives were used freely after the age of nine, relating to convictions of the duties of rulers to promote the general best interests. Little difficulty was expected in identifying such best interests – which is a reminder that children, in developing ideas, can often see a situation partially in terms of its own logic and partially in terms of sweeping generalisations.

The development of formal thinking in politics can be recognised in a child's developing abilities to deal with certain cognitive tasks. The question of 'What can he do in the formal operational stage that he can't do in the concrete-operational?' may be answered by suggesting that formal reasoning in politics, as in morality, would correspond to the appearance of a coherent perspective. This would comprise the appreciation of long-term social consequences, the ability to reason and hypothesise from premises and to use analytical modes of thought. These attributes of cognition appeared to be present to some extent in eleven-year-old children, and could also be recognised as developing in the thinking of some nine-year-olds.

Children's abilities to theorise about possible alternatives in social and political arrangements, by the age of about nine (as we have seen some of them doing), provide a significant divergence from the theory. If a child, having had certain social experiences, concludes that only particular kinds of change can express the right principles as he or she sees them, then that child is not only thinking in formal, or abstract terms, but in a philosophical mode. She, or he, is asking questions not only about the goals and the institutions of their society, but about its moral foundations. We have seen some children seize upon these kinds of questions spontaneously and begin to work on them; which is to say that they have placed themselves outside the boundaries of any 'ages and stages' categories available, and presented a discontinuity to even a flexible interpretation of Piagetian theory.

We have also seen the uses children can make of their own practical experience of relating to others and of being a member of the school community, and it has become apparent that as this 'concrete' experience is gained, so also is the ability to enter into the experiences of others, and to develop ideas and thought as a result. So it seems that any account of what is 'usable' experience for children must allow for this process taking place.

Identifying with situations through the 'here-and-now' impact of media images also appears to contribute, significantly, to children's abilities to make judgements and to ask questions about the basis of values. If we are to keep pace with this dimension of their thinking as it develops, we must examine what our society makes available to their experience, and its significance for learning. Piaget's account, while accommodating a good deal of what the children used when talking about politics and social arrangements, leaves some aspects of their thinking undescribed and un-categorised. It seems important to make the further point however, that only by using an extended analysis of cognitive growth such as Piaget provides, which gives a framework to use when observing children, can these conclusions that point to a need for further investigations be reached.

INFLUENCES ON THE DEVELOPMENT OF CHILDREN'S POLITICAL CONCEPTS

Social class, language and political understanding

To bring the relationship of language to social class into direct relevance for political concepts, with regard to its influence upon the type of thinking developed, several questions need to be considered. Firstly, do ordinary language and speech convey different meanings for different socio-economic groups? Secondly, could the children of any particular identifiable group be said to be linguistically deficient, in terms of either vocabulary or syntax, in ways likely to affect political cognition? Thirdly, are political language and information available in greater or lesser degree to any particular identifiable group?

As an exhaustive or definitive study of any of these topics might be regarded as a major undertaking, it is intended to examine the questions in the context of the data collected for this study. The question of whether ordinary language used in a political context conveys different meaning for different social groups, can be best answered by reference to children's speech. It has already been noted that the word 'work' had different connotations for different children who applied it to the Queen's activities. So much might be said of any word where, for a real description of the activity involved, the sub-skills used must be made the point of reference, and the concept analysed in terms of intentions and techniques. The choice of one facet of a wide activity for definitive attention provides one way of interpreting the world. Another is to adopt the contrary approach, and to make one word do the work of many, with the result that differentiation of related meanings becomes unclear, and the concept inaccessible to analysis. The verb 'to fight' (for votes, position, and so forth), as used by some of the Essex children, provides such an example of one word 'standing in' for a related vocabulary. By contrast, that larger, specific vocabulary was more easily accessible to the South London children, who used the terms 'elect', 'disagree', 'consult', with greater ease, and where appropriate. Some words appear to carry emotional overtones more strongly for one group than for another. The emotive response of the Essex nine-year-olds to the words 'tax' and 'taxes' was not shared by the London children.

Concern with rising prices constituted an organising concept for children from both areas, and an interesting aspect of this discussion was the different ways in which it was developed. The Essex girls at seven, eight, nine and ten all stressed the importance of prices, to the point of making this the basis of all political activity, while the London children were noticeably less affected, or emotionally involved, in this issue, preferring to regard it as one among many. Accordingly, they used a wider range of language.

The factor of emotional involvement in issues needs to be considered for its effects on the language children use. In one case of obvious strong commitment to ideas, the child concerned (age nine from the working-class group, see p. 54–6) adopted a rhetorical stance. This appeared due, not only to eagerness to persuade, but to a lack of language structures capable of organising and objectively presenting the motivating ideas. Commitment motivated her to express her ideas, by the use of extended examples from personal experiences. These enabled her eventually to transcend the 'here-and-now', and work in the future tense, reaching for causal effects and principles. This child was the agent of her own development, and achieved a sophisticated level of thought at nine years of age.

However, her discussion also illustrates a crucial point for the relating of language and political thinking; political activity exists on a time-space continuum, so thinking that is tied, conceptually or structurally, to the 'here-and-now' of present tenses or immediate concerns, is not likely to develop beyond a certain point. Limited structures of language and thought can absorb attitudes and values, accept facts and use the pronouns of solidarity. What such thought will be unable to do will be to examine critically its own origins and presuppositions and explore the relationship between facts and values or the basis of group solidarity. In other words, it will not progress fully into the formal operational stage, in terms of political cognition, until complex syntax develops.

It is apparent that, after the age of nine, some children show greater facility in using increasingly complex language structures and have more differentiated vocabulary available to them than others. As these factors are central to organising political thinking, the result is that such children are at an advantage. In addition to language, and complementing it, opportunities to acquire a wide range of information and the means of satisfying curiosity when it was aroused, appeared to be more readily available in some homes than others, and to be attached generally to a middle class environment.

Language and the family group

Much of the early literature (see Hyman 1959) on political socialisation has stressed the central and dominant role of the family in the transmission of political attitudes, emphasis being placed strongly on direct, inter-generational influences. Family habits are undoubtedly a factor here, and indeed this study provides supportive evidence in terms of political thinking. However, it is also argued that a model of political socialisation which constructs the family's role as definitive in terms of direct transmission of facts, values and affiliations, must be regarded as having serious deficiencies. It implies a passive and receptive role for children, seriously undervaluing the widely inter-active processes of individual cognitive growth. It also undervalues the individual child's personality traits, interests and abilities which result in his 'qualitative use of mind' to use Riesman's phrase (see Hyman 1959, p. 132).

Support for the view that cognitive processes in politics do develop to a considerable extent, independently of family influence, is provided by several studies. Jaros and Kolson's American study (1974) of the contrasting views of political authority figures, held by Amish, black and white children living in the same areas, concluded that general environment was more influential than the specific environment of family. Sigel and Brookes (1974) provided congruent conclusions in illustrating how young children's attitudes are influenced by government performance.

One specific question emerges initially: whether the political system becomes the family 'writ large'. This classical hypothesis, supported in the American context, by Hess and Torney (1961) for example, appears to depend to a large extent upon cultural variables. Prominent among these are the strength of political socialisation influences in the educational system, and – perhaps consequent – charisma of certain authority roles, notably the American President.

Studies such as these present questions on the role of the family in political socialisation which, it is suggested, crystallise into the conclusion reached by Kent Jennings and Richard Niemi (1968) that 'any model of socialisation which rests on the assumption of pervasive currents of parent-child value transmissions is in serious need of modification'. Some analysis of these 'pervasive currents' is of interest, in terms of investigating exactly what is transmitted. The inference generally is of a direct transfer of attitudes, orientations and ideological thinking. It is suggested on the basis of data collected during this study, and of some of the work cited, that the direct impact of events also affects children's ideas, that some political activity is directly perceived, and that this forms a category of experience.

It appears, from the evidence of children's responses, that the family influence on political thinking lies not so much in the ideological sphere directly, as in the transmission of language structures through which family groups collectively interpret information and events from the outside world. This is not to categorise families, nor attempt to allocate particular speech variants to any group. Such an undertaking is outside the scope of this work; and although there is some coherence with Bernstein's developed work in this area, which is noted with interest, proofs were not pursued. What is suggested is that a child is provided with a set of cognitive tools from the 'language and thinking' environment within the family structure of communication, and that this contribution to the growth of political understanding is one which has been insufficiently emphasised in the past.

The influence of early schooling

In this country children do not receive overt political socialisation directly through the educational system; nor do they have a presidential figure as a focus of loyalty or affection (perceived in the way that Wolfenstein and Kliman (1965) revealed American children perceived Kennedy). Neither the Prime Minister nor the Queen fill this role according to the evidence of children's written and verbal responses during this study. There is little evidence of transfer of loyalty or affection, but rather of expectation of certain standards and results, particularly from the Prime Minister.

The specific contribution of early schooling to political socialisation is to create a strong attachment to the idea of law and order, as expressed in rule-keeping, from children's biological needs for a secure and stable environment. This attitude is successfully established by an early age. It is then subject to further development, first into a desire for the approval of authority, and later into the desire to contribute to the structures of stability and authority by 'helping' or 'looking after' some aspect of school or class activities.

From the evidence of the children's responses, these habits and attitudes are often firmly established as a conscious basis for actions by the age of seven. This is a version of the process described by Hess and Torney (1967):

> The values of the adult society are transmitted through child-rearing and other practices to children who, when they become adults, reinforce and help to maintain the culture in which they live.

This process of system-maintenance appears to begin, for children in our schools, at a very early age; for it cannot only be observed in children of seven and eight, but can be articulated by that age. That is to say that more than socialisation, on a habit-forming basis, has taken place: some rational perspective appears in children's explanations and justifications. They know why they want to help in school, or hold an office, or wish to obey the rules, and reject what they consider to be excessive freedom. Learning has taken place, concepts exist and can be related to each other. For the youngest children, the concepts often take the form of conclusions drawn from intuitive thinking, but they are nevertheless based on some experience.

Children from different schools were seen to develop different ideas in the discussion groups, but their attitudes to authority, freedom and rule-keeping revealed a very similar direction of conceptual develop-ment. The common factor influencing this appeared to be the organisation of the school itself. As children's experience of social organisation and their concept of group membership are gained there, it is likely that the experience of early schooling will continue to influence future expectations and attitudes. This kind of learning is not 'mainstream' material in schools, nor taught directly; it is incidental to, but inseparable from, the purposes of schooling. As it is connected with the content, aims and context of education, there is considerable and continuing reinforcement.

Is there a sex-linked style of cognition in politics?

A proliferation of studies (see Terman and Tyler 1965, Maccoby and Jacklin 1975) have investigated the psychological possibilities of sex-linked differences in perception, and some aspects of this appear to be of interest in connection with political learning. Research on incidental learning concludes that there is no difference between the sexes' abilities to use incidental material, or to ignore it when necessary (Maccoby and Jacklin 1975, pp. 48–51).

The memory processes are also of significance for political, as any other, learning. Questions of whether boys or girls have 'better memories' lead us to ask: better memories for what? Content of learning is of basic importance, linking as it does with individual variables in levels of interest and existing knowledge, as well as with aptitudes and abilities. There is evidence that girls show rather better memory for verbal content, particularly after the age of seven (Maccoby and Jacklin 1975, pp. 56–9). However, an advantage in a memory task containing verbal content does not substantiate the notion that girls have superior memory capacities, or more efficient abilities to store and retrieve information.

There appears to be considerable support for the conclusion 'that there is no difference in *how* the two sexes learn. Whether there is a difference in *what* they find easier to learn is a different question' (Maccoby and Jacklin 1975, p. 62 and chapter 2). Accepting the above, I suggest, as a distinct possibility, that there are differences in what the two sexes learn or perceive of politics, as demonstrated by the different, and apparently sex-linked, styles of responses which were collected from the children in this study.

Fluency and quality of responses in discussion, compared between sexes

Under this heading I include abilities to present information, to provide examples or illustrations of points made, and to link items of knowledge into a sequence.

In the seven-year-olds' mixed group, the boys' responses out-numbered those of the girls, and provided information and ideas beyond the specific requirements of the question, while the girls showed no such abilities, or readiness to be extended. These girls were able to illustrate only slightly, in the course of their answers concerning the Queen, and used illustrations which were based on remembered, isolated facts. No attempts were made to connect ideas or to experiment to any extent with language or meanings, as was attempted by the boys, for example in order to account for the known actions of the Queen and to place them into a context. At eight also, boys in the mixed group took the lead in the discussion, presenting more ideas and information, generally in longer responses than the girls. Often, the girls (and one boy) appeared satisfied with a monosyllabic answer and made no effort to extend their responses.

One response which illustrates the differences between the sexes in selection of information, concerns the concept of the Queen's role and activities. This revealed a more limited view on the part of the girls, while the boys showed some ability to attend to more than one aspect of a situation. Both sets of responses were concerned with the social interactions of the Queen's role, but attention was directed to different aspects of these.

Up to the age of nine, verbal fluency and willingness to participate in discussion constituted, in mixed groups, the most obvious difference between the sexes. This might be interpreted in a variety of ways: as differences in motivation and personality traits; or as a manifestation of aggressive behaviour on the part of the boys and withdrawal on the part of the girls. It might be seen as an acceptance of sex-role stereotyping based on the perception of these attributes in sex-type models (such as children in fiction, who display a characteristic relationship between the two sexes). It can also be argued that this is an example of the characteristically different ways of thinking which were postulated by Erikson (1950). He emphasises the different ways in which children organise the sub-skills involved in problem-solving into effective procedures. Applying this construction to children dealing with ideas, it could be said that the girls produced ideas and regarded them as finished, while the boys, more attracted to the experimental role, were more likely to use ideas and to explore their potential. This suggestion can be illustrated from the conversation of the eight-year-olds: Gina's suggestion that a Prime Minister should 'have imagination' was static, in the sense of being an intuition that she could not extend, Adrian did extend to the proposal that a Prime Minister would demonstrate his imagination by suggesting, 'He'd be writing books' (see p. 42).

A further example of differences in abilities to extend ideas occurred at the end of this conversation: Gina's contention was that the difference between the tasks of being 'in charge of the British Isles' and 'in charge of all the prices' was that 'the British Isles is bigger and better than the prices'. This was specifically enlarged upon by Adrian who, unprompted, evidently felt the need to clarify. The attempt was not completely successful, as his information was inadequate, but the point to be made here concerns the *type* of thinking involved, which was explorative rather than denotive or attempting definition.

Adrian: The Queen looks after nearly the whole country – all the countries in the world, compared with the Prime Minister who just looks after England and tries – thinking whether England should stay in the Common Market.

His attempt to make criteria explicit is worth noticing, for it enabled him to clarify his thinking on a complex set of relationships, illustrating in political terms the crucial interdependence of language and thought. He further elaborated his own suggestion and consolidated his ability to use criteria.

Adrian: The Queen, she mostly travels, and, while the Prime Minister, he doesn't travel very much, he usually stays in England quite a lot of the time.

This need to elaborate or justify or explain a statement was shown, throughout the conversations, to be more typical of the boys' thinking than the girls'.

From the age of nine to eleven, children appeared to be developing an ability to think within political parameters, to stay within the conceptual area of the discipline. It was found that the boys were rather more consistent than the girls in this ability, in that the girls displayed a stronger subjective basis to thinking. An illustration of this difference in approach can be found in Marcus's discussion on political structures. This produced Sally's generalised contribution, which was to some extent a re-working of his thinking:

Q: How do you think the Prime Minister decides who's going to help him?

Marcus: He decides by getting out – the Chancellor of the Exchequer and – he's got a special name but I can't remember it. He's got the Chancellor of the Exchequer, the Foreign Minister and – the – people who look after the Education. And they all ...

Q: Special people for special jobs?

Marcus: Special people for special jobs – that are – in charge of a place.

In charge of a certain building holding certain people who do certain jobs, for different things.

Sally: He would get them all together, and he would have a few people that he thought might be good for it, and then perhaps they'd have a little vote, just to see who they thought might be best, and then he could choose himself, out of a certain number of people.

Some of the differences between the older boys and girls concerned interest in, and identification with, a public figure. Charles's orientation towards Churchill supports and reflects conclusions summarised by Hyman (1959, p. 22), concerning sex differences in ideals which apparently motivate boys towards politics at an early age. None of the girls at any stage showed a similar strength of attachment or identification towards either male or female public figures, notably not towards the Queen, nor to the leader of the Conservative party, Margaret Thatcher. In contrast, Charles's attachment was able to span the distance between his own present and his object of identification, and he could express his feelings.

The ten-year-old stage showed a widening discrepancy in the quantity of children's responses, after the near equality of the nine-year-olds. The boys were generally able to take a stronger position on most topics than the girls, both in terms of producing ideas and defending them, for example, in defining the priority of school learning over political education. A particular malleability was observed in the ten-year-old girls, not quite suggestibility in any strong sense, but rather a wish to agree and conform in interaction, and some dependence on cues. In the absence of such cues, except those which could be picked up from the boys' responses, the girls tended to take a non-committal line, choosing on occasions to echo the wording of some of the questions by way of an answer, in preference to making a positive response. This style of responding was characteristic of the ten-year-old girls in both the London and Essex groups.

For all the boys, the typical response of the ten-year-old stage emerged as an attempt to deal specifically with the question at issue, rather than to extend it. The desire to focus attention and to concentrate on limited areas appeared to be developing. This represents a point of divergence in cognitive styles between the sexes. The boys were struggling towards development of analytic capacities, while the girls' reliance on intuitive understanding limited their capacities to deal with unfamiliar subject matter.

The sex-linked differences that showed in the eleven-year-olds' responses were still linked to fluency; more responses were made by the boys than by the girls. Both sexes used examples from experience to illustrate their responses. The boys, however, used a considerably wider range of material here, and made connections for relevance in fairly lengthy digressions, such as the conservation of our natural landscape. This was a particularly interesting example, dealing as it did with remote distance; the girls' awareness of distance referred to a different part of London, an illustration nearer home. It was apparent that the boys' thinking by the age of eleven ranged more widely than the girls' in the perception of relevance and relationships, and was freer from the need to exemplify subjectively. It therefore represented the strengthening and consolidation of a basic sex-linked difference in political cognition.

This difference seems to have some of its origins in early, sex-linked perceptions of spatial relationships. These lead, in infancy, to different uses of space and therefore to different personal and social patterns of action in relation to available space and territory. Early organisation of play illustrates this point. Differences here between the sexes concern boys' apparent drive to utilise available territory, to explore and therefore internalise its nature and boundaries, either alone or in a group. In contrast, the characteristic activities of girls in early childhood appear to be much more concerned with the consolidation of personal space, which then limits the form and amount of social interaction.

As concrete actions become internalised, on Piaget's hypothesis, mental structures are formed. The nature of actions, therefore, and the ways in which patterns of actions are organised will in its turn produce sets of presuppositions for dealing with problems. In other words, it is not only the task approached in childhood as the 'concrete operation' but also the child's characteristic way of tackling it (taking it off into a corner, sharing with one friend, or a group, choosing the largest table in the classroom, being free to choose at all) that will be internalised as pre-conditions for action, and presuppositions when attached to the idea of action.

If these ways of approaching tasks are consistently found to differ between the sexes, as is suggested, then different types of pre-supposition concerning the nature of a task will ultimately be internalised. These may well remain inaccessible to analysis, but apparent in actions. Such influence will only be apparent in areas where large-scale comparison between the same activities performed by different sexes, is possible, such as voting behaviour.

Some writers have suggested a direct influence by the schools, of socialisation into sex-role stereotyping, through the content of early and continuing education, as a source of such differences of behaviour. The two theories are compatible, and capable of strongly reinforcing each other (see Lobban 1975, Byrne 1975, Wolpe 1974, Flude and Ahier (eds.) 1974).

Political learning and television

At all ages, the children questioned verbally revealed, in their answers or in spontaneous discussion, the influence of the media and particularly that of television; at seven, the larger-than-life hero – the television superman – was seen as the ideal Prime Ministerial model; asked if she knew the names of political parties, a seven-year-old girl replied, 'I don't know what it means but they do put it on a desk with writing on it – and a man speaking to you'. Some confusion occurs: having seen an MP who was deaf on television one seven-year-old boy decided: 'A Parliament party ... they help people who are deaf'.

Criticism of communication styles by boys in the seven-year-old group was based on television political broadcasts. The criteria for criticism also emanated from that source, it appeared; the expectations were of clarity and information, in the form of clear answers to questions, and the MP criticised fell below this expected standard. At seven, some children watch television news with interest.

Eight-year-olds' references to the 'money situation' and 'price situation' revealed idiomatic television language. Particular information acquired at this age showed direct links with television news reporting, as of knowledge of the Queen's travels, which are usually reported. Television does not appear to generate personal feelings about individual public figures – the ones who were liked or not liked by even the youngest children were those who had been personally seen.

The nine-year-olds were aware of television as a source of information, which often needed to be extended in discussion with parents, but which they were also capable of evaluating personally. These children possessed an impressive amount of information, but when items were discrete, or a key idea missing, as, for example, in matters of the structure of government, they were unable to make connections. There is a need for structured information, rather than mere reception of facts on a contingent basis.

For the ten-year-old girls, the 'image' reception was strong, and their interests – in Margaret Thatcher's appearance, in violence in Northern Ireland – revealed a reliance on visual memory. For the eleven-year-olds this was receding, as an increasing ability to discuss issues emerged. This was based on information and language which had obvious origins in television reporting. The only other likely general source of political and economic language and information, the schools, did not contribute to this accumulation of ideas and terminology, except on very minimal occasions.

Seen as a basic source of political information, television acquires a distinctive role in the development of children's political concepts. Dennis' (1974) reminder that:

> While the media are often listed as socialisation agents alongside parents, schools and peers, there has been little evidence for mass communication as a causal |element in a child's development of political cognitions and behaviours. [p. 391]

leads to the question of what influences or contributions television can offer. In terms of political socialisation, considered as attitude formation or reinforcement, there appears to be little scope, for political orientations can hardly be reinforced, as Dawson and Previtt suggest, where none exist (see Dennis (ed.) 1974). Also, as Connell (1974) has pointed out, an impressive array of detail is culled, but not depth: there are strong individual differences in the types of information children collect and process from this source, both cognitively and affectively.

However, the stimulation of curiosity and interest, the presentation of starting-points for further discussion within the family, and the learning of particular vocabulary and language structures appear to be a basic contribution of television. In so far as any of this happens in a particular child, it is apparent that television is a factor in the growth of political cognition.

Nevertheless, general conclusions still remain to be drawn from the evidence of children's achievements. And similarly, the factors which appear to influence their development most strongly have yet to be identified.

6

Conclusions:
some classroom implications

In developing my main arguments that children start to construct concepts of politics from about the age of seven, and that subsequently these develop through stages closely resembling Piaget's model of cognitive growth, it has been necessary to raise some complex issues which could not be pursued to their limits in the space of one book, but have been presented as aspects of my main theme. These include:

    (1) the role of language in political learning;
    (2) the influence of family and social grouping on this language and its development;
    (3) the influence of early schooling as a source of ideas from which political concepts are constructed, and the part played by certain kinds of experiences;
    (4) the question of sex-linked differences in the ways children perceive political and social issues;
    (5) the influence of media presentation on the ways in which children develop political understanding.

The point I want to make by specifying these particular areas is one that I have tried to demonstrate throughout the preceding chapters, namely that we need to know more about them, and put that knowledge to work, if we are to construct anything worth calling political education. Each is a strong – and impatient – candidate for further investigation.

    I turn now to presenting my conclusions of what the children's responses in this study seem to have established. From their written answers to questionnaires we see children, from the age of seven, possessing some basic political information, ideas and vocabulary. Between seven and eleven their written answers became progressively more specific, informative and diverse. In these terms, there was recognisable development by the age of nine, by which time many children had achieved confidence in dealing with political subject matter, and by eleven many had reached a further stage. Concepts had developed to give some perspectives on politics; that issues could be related to principles was understood, and an awareness of processes, activities and purposes was evident, implying that some coherent organisation of ideas had already taken place for these children.

At seven, many of them were able to take part intelligently in discussion about politics, to present limited but relevant information and introduce ideas; often intuitive and crude, many of their ideas had the unself-conscious vitality that children bring to the tasks that interest them. So, in addition to having quite recognisable perceptions of the nature and scope of political activity, this was a subject in which seven-year-olds could show a lively interest.

By nine, children were showing increased ability to sustain a discussion and to contribute a wider range of political topics to it. Concepts of democracy, leadership and accountability of governments were accessible to them, and some examination of these ideas was attempted, partly in the form of speculative philosophy, for the age of nine seems to be the age of the 'world view', when general theories of human nature and 'right' social arrangements flow easily. Some of these nine-year-olds were instinctive social-contract theorists; Hobbes and Rousseau were not only resuscitated but re-invented, and when ideas for re-thinking social arrangements were produced, they were justified with considerable feeling and no lack of convincing rhetoric. A capacity for social conviction and ideals became apparent, re-interpreted by some of the ten-year-olds as a belief in the power of rationality in human nature.

The ten- to eleven-year-olds produced discussions that were able to deal with aspects of competing ideologies and to understand the economic dimension in both world affairs and party politics not, obviously, in economists' terms, but as a causal effect and a dimension of policies. The eleven-year-olds no longer speculated; at this age the children were pragmatists. Party affiliations were chosen on a basis of estimating from past performances and the current credibility of individual members, which would be most likely to succeed at the polls. No affective dimension had developed in politics, for these children, in terms of loyalty towards or enthusiasm for any living public figure; their generalised loyalty and concern for the interests of 'our country' had found no personification, although concepts of leadership were demanding. A strong characteristic of children's thinking at all stages was that issues were clearly differentiated from personalities, and were of greater interest.

Piaget's stages of development in thinking were reflected in the children's development in the ways in which they held particular concepts at different ages. The idea of leadership, for example, was constructed differently, and progressively, by children of seven, nine and eleven. For the seven-year-olds, as articulated by the boys, leadership was synonymous with physical prowess; a Prime Minister should be able to perform superhuman feats and be ready to do so. Their ideas were based on fictional heroics that their leader must symbolise, but there was an attempt to connect this with reality; fantasy was used to describe ideal attributes, not simply confused with reality as adults understand it. Because to the child the 'superman' characteristics were eminently trustworthy, to demonstrate his trustworthiness, a Prime Minister must ....

The nine-year-olds chose a personification of leadership, reflecting the kind of thinking, in so doing, that can be described as 'concrete operational'. Winston Churchill became the 'concrete' means of expressing ideas that could not, as yet, be produced as abstractions. The eleven-year-olds, however, were capable of reflecting on notions of leadership and of using what they knew about Churchill to construct some perspectives on politics and history, and thus use the model for their own purposes.

The stages traceable through the children's discussions on this topic provide illustrations of thinking that is intuitive and symbolic, concrete, and finally abstract or formal, on one political topic. The record of children's conversations provides many examples of thinking coherent with Piaget's model of cognitive growth. The conclusion is that his model is confirmed and illustrated, in general terms, by the development, through consecutive and cumulative stages, of children's political thinking. However, there appear to be aspects of children's political concepts which, on the evidence of this study, are not accounted for by Piaget's model.

Some children, at the age of nine, were able to construct the possibility of alternative social and political arrangements to their present ways of life, and to justify these alternatives according to certain principles. The ability to formulate and justify such ideas is usually connected with the stage of formal operations, or abstract thought. The question therefore arises of whether, in terms of the development of social or political understanding, the stages either contract to some extent, or overlap more than in other areas. Piaget would deny that children's progress through the different stages can be speeded up in any way, for example by teaching. Nevertheless this point of divergence appeared to exist. It must therefore be concluded that the development of political cognition may be a special case, in which some contraction or unusually wide overlapping of the stages is possible. Further research here appears to be justifiable.

The age of approximately nine years appears, from the data collected, to be significant in the development of political concepts. A spurt in understanding, interest, and the ability to articulate ideas appears to take place for many children at about this age. Many of them appear to arrive on a cognitive plateau where further, less dramatic, gains and consolidation are achieved during the next two years. This finding is well documented in the study. Its particular implication is that the consolidation process might well be assisted by appropriate education at the Junior School stage. Between nine and ten years of age would appear, on these conclusions, to be the optimum time for the start of political education.

The central role of language in the development of political concepts is stressed throughout this work. It is concluded that influences upon language and language structures also have mediating effects on political thinking. These influences include the home and the school, considered to be sources of language and therefore of cognitive styles.

The most important source of children's political vocabulary was found to be television, and the majority of children involved in the study were familiar with news and current affairs programmes. From these, children gain assorted items of information which they are seldom able to place into any context of knowledge. They do not acquire affiliations from watching television; it appears to be a 'cold' medium in a very real sense for children. Personal feelings only come into play when personal contacts are involved. Language and vocabulary, therefore, remain as its basic contribution to children's political ideas – a strong contribution, in which language and images extend and reinforce each other.

Children's political vocabulary itself does not consist simply of a list of words; the ability to organise normal, everyday language in order to describe political behaviour or ideas is highly relevant. This makes meanings accessible, and questions possible, so that a child is able to work towards making the relevant concepts his own. At a certain point in this process, use of more specific vocabulary arises, as a child feels the need for it. Many children appear to have a dormant political vocabulary; they appear capable of 'living with' tacit political ideas. If these are to become explicit, the stimulus of verbal interaction appears to be both necessary and highly effective. This was concluded as a result of the discussions with the children.

This conclusion relates to a further one; that Bernstein's work on language codes and their effect on cognitive style is supported by evidence found in this study. Different uses of language, in the sense of different linguistic performance, were found to exist between different social groupings. These appeared to reflect different presuppositions and emphases in politics, together with some differences in the ways in which ideas were developed in discussion. A rigorous investigation here was beyond the scope of the present study. However, there seems to be room for further research into any direct links between language 'codes' and the development of political concepts.

The school, considered both as an authority structure and a source of aspirations and relationships, makes a pervasive contribution to early political learning. As a result of organised experiences and formalised relationships, early ideas take shape for children. These provide the basis for future development of social and political concepts. The fundamental ideas, and the situations which engender and contribute to them, are discussed and exemplified in the body of this work.

The conclusion is that a child constructs his political concepts, initially, through relating his 'here and now' world to the 'out there' political world, and finds important parts of it reflected there. In this way he brings external events under conceptual control. He also forms patterns of expectations from early schooling, which become transferred to other situations. This is the generalised process of political learning and socialisation carried by our own system at the Primary stage of education.

Education as an agency of sex-role stereotyping appears particularly to affect girls' ideas and expectations, producing attitudes which influence their development of political concepts. It is concluded, from the data collected, that girls and boys bring to political ideas different, characteristic ways of thinking and relating, and that their differences in perceptions appear to be rooted in different early experiences of play and group interaction. It was observed that girls, in single-sex groups, tended to be more self-confident and articulate in discussion, than when placed in mixed groups, while boys showed no such reactions. Further, girls appear to work from a narrower, more subjective world view than that of boys, and this mediates their styles of developing political ideas.

To establish these conclusions generally is beyond the bounds of this study. What it has shown, on the subject of sex-linked differences in political cognition, is that in this sample of children's responses there appear to be some consistent differences in thinking between the two sexes, throughout the age-range of seven to eleven years.

The idea of children's development of political concepts implies that we need to re-consider what is meant by 'political socialisation', and that acceptance of a Piagetian model raises particular questions for traditional accounts of the political socialisation process. The inter-actionist view of development emphasises children's *construction* of concepts, and the *qualities* of their thinking. Any ideas of a child's developing political mind resembling a 'tabula rasa', or blank slate, are wholly rejected.

It is concluded that the existence of such developing thought makes the question of political education an immediate one; for to ignore, educationally, a developing capacity for rationality in any area of knowledge constitutes an ideological stance *per se*. Children do acquire political information from various sources in their general environment; it is this that enables their localised, personal under-standing to expand, and this is particularly the case during periods of heightened political activity. General election campaigns for example, are very effective in stimulating children's interest in, and criticism of, political affairs and personalities although little information about parliamentary processes is available from this source. It appears necessary therefore, to raise questions of whether we would, in any other area of comparable importance, ignore the opportunity to educate children, and simply allow them to gain their information and ideas in ways contingent upon events and accidents.

SOME IMPLICATIONS FOR THE CLASSROOM

Why discuss education? My answer to this question is two-fold. Firstly, it is to point out that the data collected, and the conclusions drawn from it, provide an argument for changes in Primary education. I am suggesting that this is a powerful argument, that involves not only the provision of political education at this stage, but calls into question some of our established curriculum priorities. The second part of my answer must be the all too obvious reminder that to propose modification, where something has internal organisation and dynamics, necessitates a view of the whole. Advocating changes in these kinds of circumstances is not simply a question of bringing to them a bright new package of suggestions, and finding a convenient external peg to hang it on, but of adaptation taking place on some basic and fundamental levels. So we need to raise all the issues in education that we treat as ongoing and problematic and discuss them in relation to political learning. And to say the least, here philosophy of education gains both a further dimension and a fresh task, that of defining the kinds of questions we shall want to ask when the obvious ones (which seem to consist of adding the adjective 'political' as a prefix to 'education', so that we discuss the nature and aims of *political* education, what *political* learning and teaching are, what *political* understanding and autonomy consist of, or what *political* 'creativity' might be) begin to require expansion.

Advocating changes in what children learn also involves some necessary discussion of how they learn, and of the nature of the gap that exists between what they have learned, and what they have been able to learn as a result of schooling processes. Listening to children at different ages, in a number of localities over a period of time, is to become aware of the gap that exists for many children between their personal abilities and their school abilities, which is to say those abilities which schools recognise and seek to develop in ways that schools are able to evaluate.

At several points in the preceding chapters I have expressed an intention of returning later to the educational, or classroom, implications of a situation. This has usually been where there seemed to be something worth developing, in those kind of terms, that was not immediately relevant to the children's discussions at the time. So now I want to refer back, and use my conclusions for their usefulness in defining some problems and indicating some possibilities in classroom learning.

To turn first to the development of concepts; the indications are that children between the ages of seven and eleven are capable not only of acquiring information, but of using it intelligently, that is, to further their own enquiries and understanding. They can apply certain intellectual abilities to specific subject matter and use this to strengthen and extend their abilities. We have seen this process happening in the record of discussions, and it seems reasonable to conclude that, as a process, this is not restricted to political concepts; that the verbal stimulus to thought and ideas could, as a technique, be employed with small groups of children in order to help them 'think through' certain kinds of problems. In the Primary classroom there is a difficulty of balancing the time needed for teaching the basic skills of reading, writing and numeracy against the need for a wide range of activities for children. However, many of these activities tend to be of the 'information gathering' variety while, as yet, 'learning to think' skills are hardly recognised as a category. An accepted virtue of the 'information gathering' skills is that they tend to reinforce levels of literacy and numeracy, so that much of education in its early stages is concerned with this. Obviously, it is very necessary for children to become both literate and numerate, but there is a question of logical priorities; if children are not required to think in ways that extend their conceptual levels, until after certain standards of fluency in the basic skills are reached, then it would seem that these are being granted precedence over the development of mind. I am not suggesting that we should think in 'either/or' terms, but rather of trying to achieve some kind of balance. On the evidence of the increased capacities of those children involved in the study who were interviewed twice, the small group discussion is a powerful learning situation and stimulus. Children seemed to have been helped towards principles around which they could organise their subsequent thinking. And while at present we use this technique only with much older pupils in Secondary and Higher education, its value for younger children, as I have tried to demonstrate, can be so considerable as to be worth adopting with them.

From the evidence that I have presented of children's developing political concepts, a further implication for Primary education arises, this time concerning levels of children's achievements. It appears that we might easily be underestimating, quite considerably, our children's real abilities in some areas. I have shown that some children, at nine, are capable of abstract thinking, of forming hypotheses and making worthwhile attempts at reasoned analysis of situations. Perhaps the classroom application of this understanding, for teachers, would be the relatively simple one of keeping expectations open-ended; that is to say, looking at an individual child's own level of operating, at what he or she can do and is doing, and relating with that, on its own terms.

Starting from the premise that it is equally unfair for an able child to be left 'unstretched' as it is for a child with difficulties to be left unassisted, we assume that we know what it is for a child to be able, or to have difficulties. However, the nature of 'being able' or 'having difficulties' might well change to some extent, in the kind of learning situations that would place higher value on clear thinking and communication, and the satisfactions of exchanging ideas and making one's point of view understood. That these things are satisfactions for some children has, I hope, been shown.

The fact that some children at nine were able, and motivated, to argue for social and political alternatives has some further implications for education that are concerned with what might be described as the 'citizen' attitude. Working back from the nature of the children's statements to the feelings of involvement that prompted them reveals an attitude that approaches society and its problems in a spirit of participation. The 'ours' is definitive, applicable to country, government, debts, money and problems, the use of 'us' and 'we' almost tribal in its assumption of close-knit interests. It seems to be these feelings that have made possible the children's first participation in their society's affairs, which was to criticise. Children who argue critically about the mores and institutions of their society seem to be doing much more than simply pointing to particular questions; they are adopting a social identity, and a role characteristic of their society. They understand the game of criticising establishments and something of how to play it.

In doing so, they present a quite radical reappraisal of what has long been understood when people use the word 'childhood'; for the children I talked to were expressing claims. What they were claiming was the proper respect, as people, of having their points of view taken seriously by others. And this they were willing to extend, to each other. Nobody laughed at anyone else's ideas; nobody said anything to diminish anyone else, or competed for attention. Their way of making their claim was to argue their own rationality, or demonstrate it by giving appropriate reasons and criteria for what they said.

There are, of course, other ways of claiming consideration and expressing involvement in society than 'trying to be more mature' as one eleven-year-old put it, and it seems that the problem of how best to accommodate them, in educational terms, is going to increase. Seeing children as claimants has one or two rather interesting results; it disposes pretty finally of the models that educators have used, in a tradition of trying to capture the 'nature' of children. Making models has so fascinated educators, over a long period of time, that they have tended to replace those that become obsolete with newer versions, instead of questioning the need for them or exploring alternatives such as listening constructively to real children who have something they want to communicate. Paying attention to what children want to claim means listening to what they have to say, and this kind of listening, constructive in that it has purposes of moving discussion on, can hardly be overrated as a teaching strategy, for reasons that I hope have been made apparent. The process is not so much a 'drawing-out' of what children know, as an end in itself, as one aimed at helping them to develop skills in recognising what is relevant to an issue or what questions need to be asked, which is to say, at developing a philosophical capacity.

Some of the nine-year-olds who talked to me were already fairly adept at speculative philosophy, and some preferred to attempt a more analytical approach to things as they are. The appearance of these abilities might well be accommodated in curriculum terms by the introduction of some kind of philosophical materials for nine-year-olds, for there seems to be no reason why the ability to produce and defend argument should not be nurtured from its beginnings. An opportunity seems to exist, with this age-group, to approach political education in this way. I am not assuming the task of describing here what a political education programme for nine-year-olds might consist of. However, on the evidence I have been able to collect, the approach that seems most likely to be successful would be one that linked some examination of concepts with development in logical skills, in ways of thinking and constructing argument. If nine-year-olds are trying to do this for themselves, they are ready to accept some structure and guidelines.

So far, I have been able to use 'children' unreservedly, but it is also necessary, in referring back to my conclusions, to say something about education, learning, schooling – and girls. If my thesis is correct, and girls do develop their thinking along characteristic lines that are structured by the ways in which they organise the basic play activities of early childhood then, if we feel justified in trying to change this, the means are available. As parents, members of families and teachers, we would encourage some kinds of activities and discourage other kinds. The activities we would encourage most strongly would be those that tended to develop girls' abilities to handle complex and changing spatial relationships. The possession of complex and changing spatial relationships is characteristic of a good deal of practical activity that could be organised for these purposes, so it would seem no insuperable task to devise programmes aimed at increasing efficiency and confidence, which start as early as possible. This is not a question of re-sex-role stereotyping or any kind of manipulation of personality; it is not even the institutionalising of boys' preferences or levels of efficiency, where they seem to be different from those of girls, as norms. It is simply to say that if there are spheres of interest, ways of thinking and types of achievement that seem to be less easily available to girls, then these are discrepancies which present education with imperatives, with 'musts' and 'shoulds'.

Problems in this area would, in the first place, be the empirical ones of devising the research programmes that would test in more detail and on a larger scale my indication of a general direction. If the means of modifying children's early patterns of concept formation are as straightforward as I suggest, other considerations such as those of justifying any intervention, are inevitably involved. Arguing against this could start from premises about not interfering with what is 'natural' and 'normal', but perhaps more crucial here would be the issue of free choices for individuals.

Some people enjoy 'being girls', having girls' 'subjective' values, and 'thinking like girls'; of course, as they have not been free to choose, or able to experience other situations, this preference must be founded well and truly on irrationality, which is a state that education seeks to remedy. All things considered, there seems to be at least the makings of a problem for moral philosophers – of whom it seems that very few are girls.

From the structures of experience to the notion itself: what are we to understand by 'experience'? In spite of our inheritance from Dewey and Piaget, and our pre-fixing 'practical' to convey our own emphasis, the question is not redundant. I have raised it earlier, in connection with children's involvements with the problems and events they have not directly experenced, to argue for the value of the indirect, vicarious experience. Going a little further along that road, talking about children's 'involvement' might be a useful alternative. 'Involvement' allows for the subtle and unspecific, for empathy and imagination, without insisting on their concrete expression for legitimation as usable.

I have asserted that the question of introducing political education into the Primary school curriculum is an important and immediate one, and have presented the reasons for this at some length. That the present curriculum would be affected in a number of ways, is inevitable. In addition to the 'making room' exercise that would be necessary, political education would work as a catalyst in terms of both subjects and teaching methods, calling into question not only what should be done, but ways of doing them that have become well established and comfortable.

How long might it be, critics might well ask, before political education created its own 'faculty'? Would not some alleviation of what would soon be seen as the general ignorance of economics, and of law, be required? If it should be shown that children are able to work to some point in these areas, does it follow that they should?

The reply to this must surely be affirmative. Political education *is* the thin end of a particular wedge, but it is a wedge of necessity for living as participants in the world's affairs. And it is the reply to which a concern for the claims of education commits us, if what we mean by 'education' is understood in terms of development of mind towards the capacity for making reasoned and responsible choices.

While it is outside the scope of this book to present developed proposals for a political education curriculum, it seems feasible to indicate some possible lines of development in that area, that might be extended through both the Primary and Secondary stages in education.

There seem to be two kinds of development possible: one based on extended, experimental projects using a 'package' format and developing their own evaluation techniques; and the other placing the class teacher at the centre of the enterprise and encouraging the awareness of possibilities for political education as an element in other subjects, where this is practicable. It seems most appropriate to concentrate on the latter approach here, and to discuss possibilities in terms of the individual teacher, working with a class of children.

To return to the idea of political education as an element in other subjects, an instance of this might be seen in history. Children at the Primary stage 'see' history as a mixture of battles, heroes, assorted ways of fighting and different kinds of dress and shelter. These provide good stories, information to be looked up, basic ideas for making models and painting pictures that will be displayed in the classroom, nicely mounted and labelled, and accompanied by pages of careful writing, describing it all. A classroom can be a visual delight, children absorbed and working to produce results. What might be questioned is what is being gained in terms of intellectual skills linked to historical concepts. Further, what attitudes and expectations are children developing, from the extended story of physical conflict and aggression as the traditional forms of problem-solving? What alternative opportunities are being lost?

One alternative might be to change the focus on events, to show other problem-solving skills at work. I am thinking of the occasions in human affairs when violence has been avoided, negotiations been successful, demands moderated and tolerance employed. Perhaps it would not be too difficult to analyse such situations for their dynamics, and present their effects as the real successes in human terms. It seems possible that other subjects might provide similar possibilities, and that teachers might well be helped to recognise and use them.

To be successful, this way of working, and any similar exercises, must be seen to be in the children's interests and of value to society. So, justifications of that nature, extrinsic to political education, are needed. Without them, the question of 'Why do this?' becomes as difficult to answer as the related question of 'Why educate?'. The problem is not to find answers, but to give an answer that takes all possible points of view into account.

The justification for political education that does this on a global scale, stems from a basic proposition: that whatever else, as individuals or groups we might regard as desirable, we prefer our own continued survival to extinction, as a human community. And to this end, we are concerned for world peace. It follows that those activities which tend to promote peace, and strengthen the likelihood of our survival, will be the ones we value and support. Those activities are not always easy to specify, or even to recognise, in advance. Sometimes it is only in retrospect that we understand the significance a course of action had, at a given moment. This being so, it seems all the more important that a society should make some commitment to, and investment in, activities that can be specified and used intentionally, to promote peace. Education for peace must be a strong candidate here.

If we can conceive of such a direction for education, it could hardly be conceived of as credible without some provision for political education. The question might then be asked of how the notion of links between political education and constructive ways of promoting peace through education can be substantiated. Put another way, what has political education to offer in this respect?

Evaluation must be, initially, in terms of what political education sets out to do. So some kind of general agreement about this, in terms of principles, seems necessary. This is not to say that a formula or any set of universal guidelines is necessary, or even desirable. Rather, the identification of what knowledge, skills and values are likely to be most useful will be a matter for public discussion and consensus, not for personalities and preferences. The task of political education, if it is to have any claim on the school curriculum, would essentially be to establish the learning situations in which individuals gained the knowledge, developed the skills and understood the demands of values that are publicly acceptable.

Can we specify these situations? There seem to be two general approaches to build on: a 'constitutional' or structural emphasis to teaching about politics; and a concept-based approach. Most useful for classroom purposes would be a combination of these. Informing children about the structures and processes of politics would have little meaning in a vacuum; to fill this, the human dimension of purposes and their ideological expression is necessary.

How such content can be processed, organised and presented effectively to different age-groups and ability levels becomes a question for syllabuses, and it may well be that these will work best as a succession of spirals, which is to say that material presented in an understandable form to children fairly early in their school life will be returned to at a later stage, its early foundation extended and built upon. An example of what might happen may be useful here: take the idea of a law. As early as seven, as we have seen, children not only know what a law is, some of them are able to hold the concept of a 'bad law'. This implies not only the ability to differentiate between the law and the over-arching moral principle by which to judge it, but to decide whether a law is justified in terms of the principle it is supposed to serve.

Given that children generally are capable of this understanding, that is, they can use the expression 'a bad law' with meaning, then information about the processes of making laws – which is in effect the rules of a particular kind of game – would not be beyond their comprehension. For a teacher to present the 'journey' of a law should, on the evidence which was presented earlier of the younger children's capacity for discussion, give rise, even with first-year juniors, to sufficient interpolations along the lines of: 'But what happens if ...'; 'Supposing they ...'; 'But can they ...' – and so on, for many of the discussion points to be dealt with.

From such fundamental beginnings, children can be helped to

develop the kind of knowledge that will enable them, at the Secondary stage, to work easily in such areas as comparative constitutional arrangements, rather than simply assimilate information. Without the earlier stages, this might well be the limits of their involvement in provisions made solely for the Secondary stage. For there is a difference between extending knowledge of familiar areas, and starting from scratch in terms of the quality of involvement and participation possible.

What kind of significance does a topic such as the study of constitutional arrangements have for children, in the long-term? The understanding of how a society lives by its political assumptions, how these arose and came to be expressed in its constitution, is to understand how it relates with its own past. Such understanding will include awareness of how all this influences the present, through defining the kinds of choices that are available to groups. Public understanding in this area seems at present to be minimal. To cite a very obvious example, very little real understanding exists here of even such a well-publicised event as a presidential election in the United States. And no doubt the converse could be stated. This is surprising, to say the least, particularly between two countries where information is perfectly accessible. The obvious conclusion is that this kind of information has not been, at any stage, presented as interesting or useful. Returning to the question of its significance, one way of answering that question is to consider the kinds of expectations that one society can have of another. Only in an awareness of what is possible, of where the real power of the system is located, and of the strength of particular attitudes, can realistic expectations be held by one group of another.

These problems exist not only on an international scale. It is a truism that detailed awareness of our own political arrangements and institutions is not a highly developed characteristic of our society. So there is a good deal of work to be done if, in the future, we are going to be able to develop children intelligently and constructively as an electorate. If the habits of the past are followed, such development will be in the nature of acquiescence, rather than activity. Acquiescence, or consent to government, is a concept that bears examination not least for its relationship with other democratic concepts, particularly to the notion of the accountability of governments. How would political education, linked with the idea of promoting the intention of peace, examine such concepts?

The way forward implies the necessity of scrutiny and revitalisation by asking questions, not of what we have come to understand by them, as if that were the end of the road, but of how we can put them to work. Political education itself sets a problem for notions of responsibility and accountability; for where would responsibility for establishing it lie? There seems to be no logical reason why this should be the sole responsibility of teachers and schools. We might want to consider whether our Members of Parliament, as the local experts and professionals, should bear any responsibility, not for the nature of what could be provided, but for the provision itself.

In terms of the teachers' contribution, there are some practical constraints on time and organisation to be considered. While occasional sessions with small groups may be possible, the realities of the classroom usually mean that most teachers, for much of the time, look for the kind of activities that can involve all the children in a class in some way. Some useful strategies here might include utilising what the media can offer in the form of news or the reporting of specific issues in which a class might decide to take a special interest, newspaper and magazine articles, and broadcasts from the House of Commons itself, as well as any local political activity.

In some ways, political education at the present time stands in a similar relationship to the school curriculum as sex-education has, in the recent past. There are some obvious similarities in attitudes towards the two, for similar kinds of reasons. And there are the same reasons for starting children's education in the areas in question before the age of puberty, when ideological, as well as emotional considerations, arise. From the comparison with sex-education there arises the question of links with the schools' provision for morally educating children, and a further comparison with religious education. In this area, where the claim to 'teach about', not convert, is a solid one, consideration of its value has become linked with the necessity for providing moral education.

I would argue a role for political education here, in its emphasis on examining the working of social concepts – freedom, equality, questions of rights, relationships with authority – and their meaning within a society. Both public and private morality make use of the central concept of respect for the status of the individual. So there is a case to be made for political education, in its direct application of the concepts of moral discourse 'writ large', having the stronger pragmatic claim to educate morally.

At the present time, our public ideas about political education and the Primary school curriculum seem to be, to a great extent, at the 'pre-conceptual' and 'intuitive' stages of thinking. If this is so, then we might expect shortly to move into a stage of 'concrete' activity, in the form of an increase in experimental situations, with a consequently greater scope for discussion and exchange of information. My concern has been to argue, and to demonstrate, that the 'readiness' condition for this exists in many children, requiring simply the opportunities for expression.

This issue in education goes beyond the classroom and the school in its objectives; for the commitment is not only to help children to understand the world, but to help them develop the knowledge, skills and powers of reflection that will best enable them to preserve it for themselves.

Appendix

THE QUESTIONNAIRES

The following 38 questions were used in the questionnaires.

1. What is the Prime Minister's name?

2. What do you think he does?

3. Does the Queen do any work?

4. What does she do that you know about?

5. Do you know what a law is? (Underline 'a rule', 'a game', 'a story' or 'don't know'.)

6. Is there a form captain or leader in your class?

7. Would you like to be a form captain?

8. Why?

9. Would you like to be a monitor?

10. Why?

11. What are laws and rules for?

12. Are there any laws that you would like to make, if you could?

13. Is it important to keep the school rules?

14. Why?

15. Would it be nice to do just as you like all the time?

16. Have you ever voted for anything?

17. Do you know what that means?

18. Do you know what Parliament is?

19. Do you know what people do there?

20. Do you know how people come to be there?

21. People who help to make the laws are called Members of Parliament. Do you think we could all do that if we wanted to?

22. Do you think only some special people could?

23. Do people who make the laws need to be very clever?

24. More clever that most people?

25. Do they need to be good?

26. Do they need to be as good as most other people?

27. What do you think politics is about?

28. What do you think political parties do?

29. Why do we have different parties?

30. Do you think the different parties agree about most things?

31. What kind of things might they not agree about?

32. How do we know a good Prime Minister?

33. What kind of things should a Prime Minister do?

34. What kind of things would a bad Prime Minister do?

35. What should happen to a bad Prime Minister?

36. How does a Prime Minister decide what to do?

37. Does anyone help him?

38. Do you know what the House of Commons and the House of Lords are?

These questions can be classified into four sets (1–10; 11–17; 18–26 and 27–38) on the basis of the kinds of concepts, or the attitudes they were intended to explore. Thus questions 1–10 are concerned with children's possession of basic information and attitudes towards the kinds of authority and responsibility accessible to them in the classroom. Questions 11–17 introduce a requirement for judgements to be made of familiar situations, probably for the first time, in connection with ideas of authority and freedom. The questions on voting follow, as any experience the children have of voting is usually linked to either choosing games, in peer groups, or filling classroom offices. Questions 18–26 require more specific political information than the earlier questions, and investigate to some extent children's attitudes towards elite groups and their accessibility. The final group, 27–38, make complex demands, and with the exception of question 38, require answers in terms of evaluative thinking in politics. The final question makes the strongest demand for specific information, and presents an opportunity for children to relate whatever they are able on the subject. There is some gradation of difficulty between the sets of questions, and between individual questions in each set. It was intended that all the participant children should be able to produce answers of some kind, while the more able would have the opportunity of presenting, or even extending, their ideas.

Select Bibliography

Beard, Ruth M. (1969) *An Outline of Piaget's Developmental Psychology* London: Routledge and Kegan Paul, see p. 17.

Bernstein, Basil (26th February 1970) 'Education Cannot Compensate for Society' in *New Society*, pp. 344–7.

Bernstein, Basil (1971) 'On the Classification and Framing of Educational Knowledge' in Michael F. D. Young (ed.), *Knowledge and Control* London: Collier Macmillan.

Bruner, Jerome S. (1973) *Beyond the Information Given* London: George Allen and Unwin.

Byrne, E. M. (1975) 'Inequality in Education – Discriminal Resource-allocation in schools?' in *Educational Review*, June 1975, pp. 179–91.

Chomsky, N. (1967) 'The Formal Nature of Language' in E. Lenneberg (ed.), *Biological Foundations of Language* New York: John Wiley, pp. 397–442.

Connell, Ralph W. (1974) *The Child's Construction of Politics* Melbourne: Melbourne University Press.

Dennis, Jack (1974) *Socialisation to Politics* New York: John Wiley, pp. 391–2.

Erikson, E. H. (1950) *Childhood and Society* New York: Norton.

Hess, Robert D. and Torney, Judith V. (1967) *The Development of Political Attitudes in Children* Chicago: Aldine, see pp. 7, 95–101, ch. 2.

Hyman, Herbert (1959) *Political Socialisation* Glencoe: The Free Press, pp. 1–16.

Jaros, D. and Kolson, K. L. (1974) 'The Multifarious Leader: Political Socialisation of Amish, 'Yanks', 'Blacks' ' in R. Niemi (ed.), *The Politics of Future Citizens* London: Jossey Bass.

Jennings, K. and Niemi, R. (1968) 'The Transmission of Political Values from Parent to Child' in *American Political Science Review*, vol. 62.

Kohlberg, L. (1971) 'Stages of Moral Development as a Basis for Moral Education' in C. M. Beck, B. S. Crittenden and E. V. Sullivan (eds.), *Moral Education: Interdisciplinary Approaches* New York: Newman Press.

Lobban, G. (1975) 'Sex-role in Reading Schemes' in *Educational Review*, June 1975, pp. 202–9.

Maccoby, E. E. and Jacklin, Carol N. (1975) *The Psychology of Sex Differences* London: Oxford University Press, see pp. 48–51, 56–59, 62, ch. 2.

Mealings, R. J. (1963) 'Problem Solving in Science Teaching' *Educational Review*, vol. XV, pp. 194–207.

Mussen, Paul H., Conger, John J. and Kagan, Jerome (1969) *Child Development and Personality* (Third edition) New York: Harper & Row.

Polanyi, M. (1958) *Personal Knowledge* London: Routledge and Kegan Paul.

Polanyi, M. (1969) *Knowing and Being* London: Routledge and Kegan Paul.

Sigel, R. S. and Brookes, M. (1974) 'Becoming Critical About Politics' in R. Niemi (ed.), *The Politics of Future Citizens* London: Jossey Bass.

Stubbs, M. (1976) *Language, Schools and Classrooms* London: Methuen, pp. 42–50.

Terman, L. M. and Tyler, L. (1954) 'Psychological Sex Differences' in L. Carmichael (ed.), *Manual of Child Psychology* (Second edition) New York: John Wiley, ch. 17.

Warnock, Mary (1973) 'Towards a Definition of Quality in Education' in Richard S. Peters (ed.), *Oxford Readings in Philosophy: Philosophy of Education* Oxford: Oxford University Press.

Wolfenstein, Martha and Kliman, Gilbert (eds.) (1969) *Children and the Death of a President* Gloucester, Mass: P. Smith.

Index

Details of our complete list are available in the following areas:
Politics and Sociology, Social Policy, Education, Economics,
Soviet Studies and Women's Studies. Copies of catalogues and
further information on particular titles can be obtained from
Promotion Services Department, Martin Robertson and Co.
Ltd., P.O. Box 87, Oxford OX4 1LB.

SUBJECT WOMEN

ANN OAKLEY

The position of women in contemporary western culture is
more complex than ever before. Ann Oakley's book is a powerful analysis of what it means to be female in society today.

'An exciting, bracing and at times very inspiring book.'
Marina Warner, THE SUNDAY TIMES

*'The book should make converts to feminism as well as providing
information for women who are already feminists . . . it is admirable
– clear, sane and reliable.'*
Janet Radcliffe Richards, THE GUARDIAN

THE ULTIMATE RESOURCE
JULIAN SIMON

The real shortage is people.

So argues Julian Simon in this provocative and lively attack on those who sound alarms against population growth and resource use. He challenges conventional beliefs about the scarcity of energy and natural resources, the pollution of the environment, the effects of immigration and the validity of forecasts about population change.

'*The book is thought provoking in the best sense of this hackneyed term. Altogether this is a very good book.*'
Professor P. T. Bauer, LONDON SCHOOL OF ECONOMICS

THE OTHER PRICE OF
BRITAIN'S OIL

W. G. CARSON

Britain is now reaping the benefit of the great oil and gas bonanza in the North Sea but at what price?

In this major new study W. G. Carson argues that the price paid in terms of death and injury to oil workers has been much too high. Has the regulation of safety and enforcement of existing legislation been downgraded in the rush to get the oil out quickly?

The author convincingly shows that the popular image of offshore danger is at odds with the reality of North Sea oil exploration. Drawing on detailed evidence from accident files and other sources he reveals that the vast majority of casualties in the North Sea result from relatively mundane and easily controllable factors; factors familiar to anyone concerned with the regulation of industrial safety in general.

The Other Price of Britain's Oil confronts the less creditable – and less publicised – side of the North Sea success story.

THE POLITICS OF POVERTY
DAVID DONNISON

From 1975 to its dissolution in 1980, David Donnison acted as chairman of the Supplementary Benefits Commission, working on the administration and reform of one of the most important, and contentious, set of social measures for alleviating poverty in Britain.

This book tells the inside story of what was achieved and how, and gives a unique insight into the policymaking process in British government.

The Supplementary Benefits Commission is no more, but the problems of poverty and deprivation are more in evidence than ever. David Donnison uses his knowledge and experience to make an acute analysis of the experience of poverty in Britain today, and he puts forward a positive programme of measures to combat it and to try and create a more just and equal society.